Hand Spun

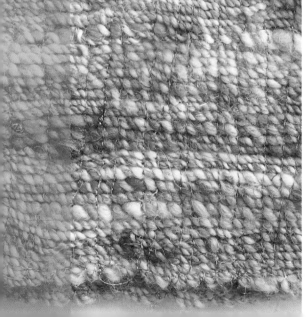

Hand Spun

New Spins on Traditional Techniques

Lexi Boeger

Quarry Books
100 Cummings Center, Suite 406L
Beverly, MA 01915

quarrybooks.com • craftside.typepad.com

© 2012 Quarry Books
Text, photography, and illustrations © 2012 Lexi Boeger

First published in the United States of America in 2011 by
Quarry Books, a member of
Quayside Publishing Group
100 Cummings Center
Suite 406-L
Beverly, Massachusetts 01915-6101
Telephone: (978) 282-9590
Fax: (978) 283-2742
www.quarrybooks.com
Visit www.Craftside.Typepad.com for a behind-the-scenes peek at
our crafty world!

10 9 8 7 6 5 4 3 2 1

ISBN: 978-1-59253-762-4
Digital edition published in 2012
eISBN: 978-1-610581-943

Library of Congress Cataloging-in-Publication Data available

Design: Deborah Dutton
Photography and Illustrations: Lexi Boeger
Design and patterns by Lexi Boeger, unless otherwise noted.
Text on pages 22; 34; 50; 68; 74; 78, excerpted from *Intertwined*,
    © 2008 Quarry Books.

Printed in Singapore

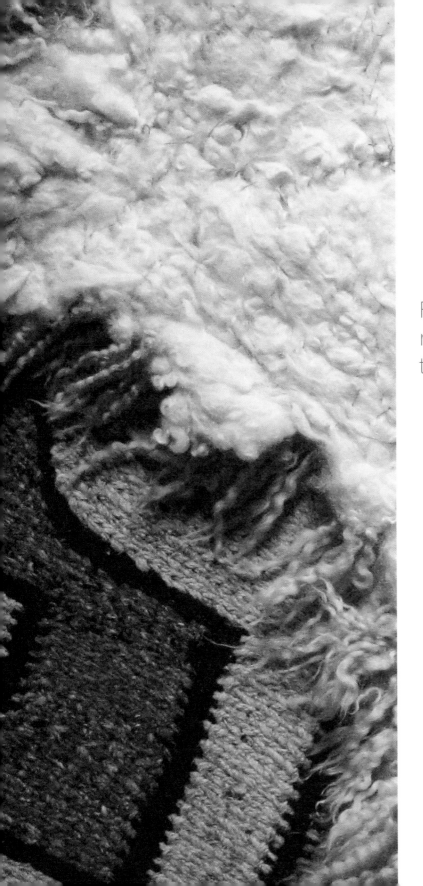

For Susan Boeger, without whom none of this would be possible—the best mom ever!

contents

Remember, spinning should be fun!

introduction

This book, *Hand Spun* is the black sheep looking back at its roots and knowing that, though its difference makes it stand out, it's a sheep after all—it's only on the surface that it is anathema to the flock. The art-yarn movement speaks to the black sheep in us all. It allows us to feel like we are ditching the flock and running as fast as our little black hooves will take us over the grassy hill that we can't see beyond, where we can do what we want, *baa* with the wolves, eat only dandelions, and opt for a night under the stars in place of the safety of the barn. But ultimately, the grass is green, no matter what side of the fence you jump over.

This book is a testament to our roots, an acknowledgment that in this craft things don't start at the beginning, they start at the core, and spin out from there. Whether you are a traditional spinner or a barely definable fiber-artist spinner, the core from which we all work from is the same. The roots are in the fiber and the very basic ways in which we turn those fibers into yarn. Art yarn is merely tradition exaggerated. But if you look closely, you can see the white sheep in the bloodlines.

During my first exposure to hand spinning, I had the distinct fortune to be placed in front of dirty, unskirted raw fleece. At that time I barely had an inkling of what spinning was and certainly had no notion of where it might take me. Art yarn did not exist at that time and there were only a few novelty styles around. So it was not the bright colors or the wild styles that got me. It was that fleece, so basic and so straightforward, and sorting through it for the piece that would become my first yarn—I came up with an ounce of fiber and lanolin under my skin that never came out.

Preparing fiber from scratch and spinning it into yarn is an intimate process that connects the spinner with the long history of spinning. There is a legacy within this craft which is everyone's to inherit. All you need to do to claim it is to take the steps along the core path that starts at the barn and goes from there to wherever you want. But in starting with the tradition, you can see what makes spinning so engaging, and so familiar. Familiar because the core processes of spinning have been repeated throughout the history of humankind, over and over. It has become a blood knowledge.

So here in *Hand Spun*, we will look at some traditional processes and techniques. We will learn them. We will appreciate them. And then, we will turn them on their ear.

Owen Poad, wheel maker and owner of Majacraft in New Zealand

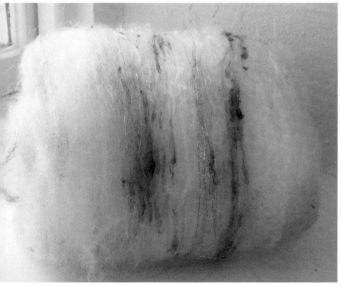

above: Mohair carded with hand-dyed silk noil, wool in yellow and blue, and re-claimed metallic threads.

right: When the fiber has been prepared in a beautiful or interesting manner, the yarn will look good, even spun in the most basic of ways.

Chapter 1

Fiber Preparation: Dyed-in-the-Wool

The real key to creative yarn making does not lie solely in the spinning, it comes much earlier than that. Creativity is dyed-in-the-wool, so to speak. That idiom comes from the process of textile making, referring to the fact that if you dye the fibers earlier in the process, the hues become deeper, more ingrained, and less likely to fade or change. The same holds true for applying your creative ideas to the yarn-making process. Because yarn making is just that— a complete process, of which the actual spinning is just one step. If you want your yarn to be creative to the core, you have to start at the beginning. There are five basic steps in the process of yarn making, all of which provide an opportunity to influence the final outcome. First is the growing of the fiber: raising fiber animals and growing or collecting plant or other materials. Second, the treatment of the raw fiber or fleece: skirting, washing, and scouring. Third, color treatment: dyeing. Fourth, fiber preparation: picking, carding, and combing. And finally, the spinning of the fiber. The earlier you can make creative decisions in the process, the more the artistry will be an inherent part of your yarn. "Dyed-in-the-wool" is a term used when people have a characteristic or belief that is so deeply set in them that it is inseparable from their very nature. In order for your individual artistic perspective to be as powerful and authentic as possible, you will want to have a hand in the process from the very beginning.

From the Ground Up

You can make bad yarn from good fiber, but it's hard to make good yarn from bad fiber. The importance of starting with good fiber is imperative. Good can mean anything from high quality in terms of grade and being interesting, beautiful, unusual to look at, or politically good in terms of how it was raised and the farming practices employed. Whatever your focus, it is important that you consciously choose your fiber for its goodness, however you define that for yourself. Feeling invested in and proud of the materials you work with will ultimately shine through in your final creation.

Hand spinners have always been close allies with the small farmer, but even more so today. Thanks to a huge increase of interest in hand spinning, combined with the Internet, we are experiencing the boutique-ifying of the fiber farm. And though this may make some cringe, ultimately it is a positive advance for both farmer and spinner. Americans are becoming obsessed with "going small." From independent coffee roasters to local-only produce, we like to feel connected to what we're buying. Simultaneously, with the increase of spinners on the Internet, fiber producers began to establish websites (in what might be considered the sweetest marketing plan ever) featuring the home-photographed faces of one fiber creature after another. The animals' names are proudly printed under each photo followed by a short bio, including details about their habits, personalities, and of course, their fiber quality. A spinner can try out Marbella's spring fleece and if she likes it, she can ask for it by name the next year along with an update of the animal's growth and antics for the year. The symbiotic relationship between farmer and spinner is a wonderful one and creative spinning is particularly suited to benefit both. As so many creative spinning styles are designed for the express purpose of bringing out the inherent beauty and specific qualities of each individual fleece or fiber, unique spinners want equally unique fiber.

Natalie Redding

Namaste Farms
Temecula, California

As I sit across the table from Natalie Redding in a pub, I struggle to reconcile this tall, beautiful, long-haired, Prada-boot-clad former model with her tales of shearing sheep twice her size, her favorite inoculation techniques, and the ins and outs of handling a thirty-five-foot (10.7 m) trailer full of award winning Angora goats. She looks like a California princess but curses and drinks like a wayfaring sailor. I like her right off, and not just because we have an affinity for the same cheap American beer. Her stories about breaking into the insular world of raising competition fiber animals and the great resistance she met has struck a real chord with me. In appearance, demeanor, and life experience she was so different from her fellow farmers they simply assumed she wasn't one. She was a decidedly nontraditional person entering a very traditional field. It's a discomfort with change and a fear of losing the stability of traditions that cause people to become reactionary. And the same is true of Natalie's experience. Natalie was initially viewed as an outsider, but actually she was a farmer through and through. She just did it with more style and sass than most people were ready for. And since she didn't look the part, she had to earn respect the old fashioned way; by working hard and proving herself. Natalie, with a master's degree in animal science from Cal Poly, San Luis Obispo (with an emphasis in molecular biology), has since established a breeding program on her farm for world-class mohair. From breeding decisions to shearing, it's her elbow grease that has recently taken Namaste Farms goats to the top. The proof is in the pudding as they say, and as I sit here holding a 9" (23 cm) long lock of the most lustrous mohair I have ever seen, all I can say is, "Respect. Natalie, you earned it!"

Q and A: Lexi and Natalie

In addition to her prized goats, Natalie alternately works with, looks after, or tends to five children, one husband, a herd of Wensleydale, Gotland, and Racka sheep, several head of cattle, two horses, alpacas, llamas, geese, peacocks, turkeys, and 600 chickens.

Is agriculture a lifestyle you were raised in or did you come to it on your own?

I was born with a deep attachment to animals. My father raised bird dogs and he bought me a pony named Buck. Ole Buck lived true to his name and I landed face down in the dirt many times. In fact, he shattered my elbow, broke the growth

plate, and dislocated the joint twice. It didn't matter, I loved him, and knew my life would be dedicated to animals.

You don't fit the standard farmer profile. Did you experience resistance or encouragement when you first entered the field?
When I first started, people were not very nice. I was not warmly welcomed at the first show I went to, and was even told I should change the way I dressed. I was in tears several times during that week. Years later, I was asked to be in a magazine about my shearing technique, I placed an ad in the magazine, and actually received hate mail. It was devastating. But once people learned that I was educated, did everything myself, and could produce (not just buy) winning animals, they started being nice to me.

What goals have you set for your animals and have you met them?
My goals were to buy the best animals from the best breeders. I was fortunate to have had deep pockets at the time and that seemed to outrage people. They didn't see it as supporting other breeders, they saw it as taking a shortcut. My thinking was that these top breeders have been doing this for many years—I'll pay a lot for their stock, but I will save in the long run. Once I bought winning animals, I just bred the best to the best. Now, I breed my own champions.

What have been your biggest success and your biggest failure? What did you learn from each?
If you talk about success in terms of personal satisfaction, it would be that the top breeders in my field have respect for me. If you are talking about show titles, I have animals that have earned many. My favorite is the 2009 CAGBA National Grand Champion Angora Goat, Cloudspun Samba. Looking at all the trophies and ribbons give me confirmation that, even though my original philosophy made people angry, it was the right thing for me to do.

As far as failures, I can honestly say I don't think there is one. Maybe it is because if I see something is not going to work, I "stop the bleeding." I don't hang on for the outcome; I refocus my energy.

What traits do you consider the most important when breeding for spinning fiber?
This is a fantastic question. By far, the single most important thing to me is a fine-fleeced animal that has longevity in producing fineness. For example, Angora goat fleece coarsens as the goat ages. I tell people not to let a breeder show you their kids and yearlings to see how good a fleece is, go to their older goats. The older goats will tell you everything you want to know about this person's stock. Personally, I want a goat that produces yearling fleeces at 7 years of age. This is not impossible; I have several does that actually do this. It is the result of many years of selective breeding and incredibly detailed record keeping by the original breeders (Sharon Chestnutt and Dr. Fred Speck). It is so important to look at the long-term value of a goat.

What would you say to other spinners considering taking the leap from buying fiber to raising their own? Is it worth it?
This sounds really rough, but I feel that if you can't euthanize an animal yourself when it is suffering, you have no business owning them. Too often people think what I do is so romantic, but they don't really have the stomach for some of the realities and challenges that go along with it. If you have an animal hamstrung by a coyote at 2:00 a.m., you have to know you can pull the trigger. The animal is counting on you to do it at that moment, before it suffers. This is what we do as responsible livestock owners.

A person will never be able to make enough money from fleeces to offset other costs. Hay and grain prices are high, and animal maintenance is backbreaking work. I would have the animals even if it weren't my business. I love them, and I love them enough to never put myself first and to never let them suffer.

How to Wash (or Not) Raw Fleece

Starting with a raw fleece can be one of the best experiences in spinning. Once you get comfortable dealing with and handling raw wool, heavily processed commercial roving begins to seem, well, shallow. Having a hand in every step of the yarn-making process will bring depth and authenticity to your experience. All spinners have their favorite way of processing fleece; the following are methods I have found to work well.

Warning!

Do not agitate the fleece during the washing process or it will cause the fleece to felt! Handle it gently at all times; don't run the water while the fleece is in the tub!

Scouring Fleece

Scouring is the term for washing fleece to remove lanolin, sweat residue (suint), dirt, and vegetable matter. Some people do this process in a washing machine but I do not recommend this method. I have seen enough twisted, half-felted fleece come into my class to realize that not all washing machines are created equal. If you don't set the dial right at the very beginning of the spin cycle and the machine begins to spin before the water has drained out, it will create a whirlpool effect. The fleece will twist in the current, start felting from the agitation, and come out looking like something you might have seen at a Queen concert. (Please see "Washing-Machine Boa" on pages 107–108 for how to capitalize on this.) Play it safe and use a utility sink or tub to wash your fleece.

1. Lay your fleece out on the ground and skirt it. Remove all unusable fleece from the edges, and pull out fiber that is severely matted or dung-covered.
2. Fill a utility sink, washbasin, or tub with very hot water and a ¼ cup (60 ml) of liquid degreasing dish soap.
3. Do yourself a favor, and invest in a sturdy wire basket for this process; you won't regret it! Submerge the wire basket in the tub, add enough fleece to cover the surface of the water, and gently submerge it into the soapy water. Note: Don't over-fill your tub with fleece, the fleece needs to have enough exposure to the water to clean it.
4. Let the fleece soak for two hours.
5. Lift the basket with the fleece out of the water and set aside; allow the water to drain from the fleece while you refill the tub.

(Continued)

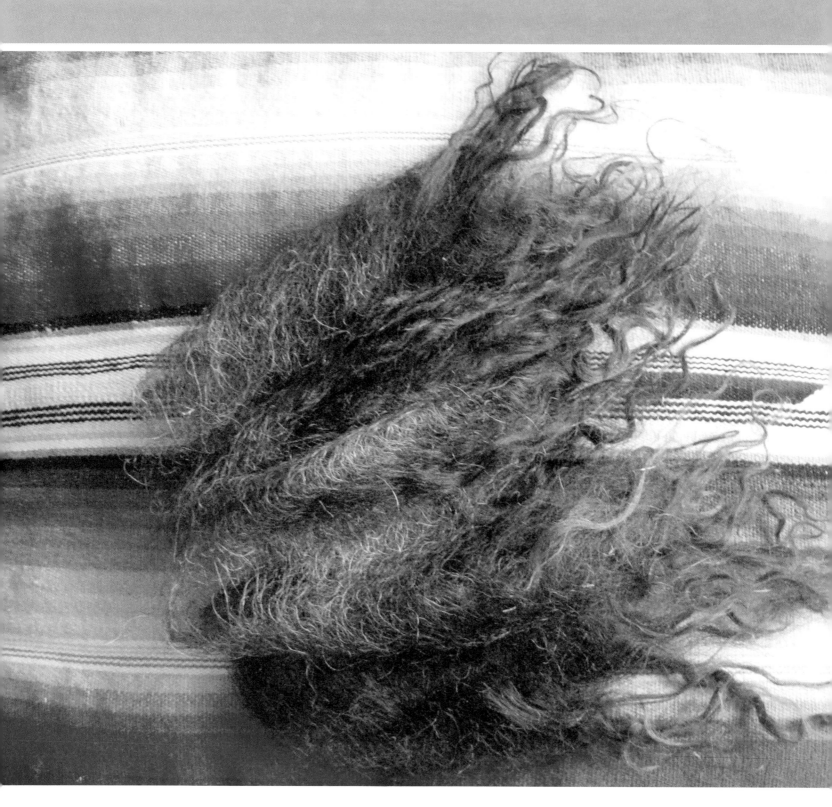

6. Refill the tub with hot water.
7. Submerge the basket and fleece gently.
8. Let soak for thirty minutes.
9. Repeat the thirty-minute soaks until the water runs clean.
10. Add 1 cup (240 ml) of vinegar to the last bath.
11. Remove the basket with fleece from the water, and gently place the fleece into a top-loading washing machine. Set to the spin cycle to remove excess water.
12. Remove the fleece and lay out to dry. (The wire basket is also handy for drying! Set it out where air can get underneath, and the fleece will dry quickly.)

Fleece Preparation for Spinning in the Grease

It's surprisingly fun to spin greasy fleece. You can comb the locks out in advance or just pick them apart by hand and spin directly from the lock. Note: Greasy wool can wreak havoc on your carder. Either dedicate an old carder to this purpose or stick with the combs. The following is a process for getting the suint, dirt, and vegetable matter out before spinning, but leaving the lanolin in. Do not add soaps or detergents!

1. Soak the fleece in a cold-water bath overnight (or for about six hours during the day), and then place it in a tepid-water bath for about thirty minutes.
2. Repeat the cold-to-tepid process until the water runs clean.
3. Remove the fleece and spin out excess water in a top-loading washing machine set on the spin cycle.
4. Let set to dry.

Let's Get Dirty!

If you want to skip the scouring process entirely, simply skirt your fleece, and spin directly from the locks. Raw fleece not only has lanolin but sweat residue, vegetable matter, and dirt. This doesn't bother me—in a sensory way it feels close to the barn and the animal, but it may be an acquired taste! All of these things can be washed out once the fiber has been spun into yarn. (See page 84 for yarns spun from raw fleece.)

Note

Many spinners prefer not to wash alpaca before spinning. It does not have lanolin to begin with and the vegetable matter, as well as a fair amount of the dust and dirt, will fall out during carding. Any dirt that remains can easily be removed by washing the final yarn.

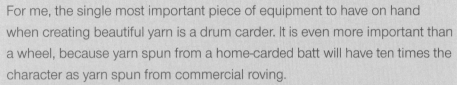

Carding

For me, the single most important piece of equipment to have on hand when creating beautiful yarn is a drum carder. It is even more important than a wheel, because yarn spun from a home-carded batt will have ten times the character as yarn spun from commercial roving.

I would rather have a drop spindle and a drum carder than a fantastic wheel and commercial roving. Hand carders are okay, but it takes a lot of time and effort for me to produce a small amount of useable fiber.

A drum carder is a substantial investment, but in the long run it will save you plenty of money by allowing you to purchase raw or uncarded fleece which you can process yourself. In addition, hand-processed fiber retains much more texture and loftiness.

Traditionally, carding has been used to prepare the fiber for spinning by separating the locks and grooming them in one direction. The goal was to remove every little lump and generate a fiber that would spin evenly and quickly. The carder had always been an instrument for taming the fiber, but no more! A drum carder in the hands of a creative thinker can be a tool for unleashing the most stunning and unusual qualities from a wide range of fibers and materials.

Think of a carder as a mixer rather than a tamer, and a batt as a creation in and of itself. All of your color, texture, and material choices can be put together in the carding process. The rest is easy . . . just spin!

Thick-and-thin single-spun yarn from a crazy-carded batt. The yarn includes wool, mohair, sequins, recycled silk, cut threads and yarns, shredded money, semi-felted wool, silk noil, Lincoln locks, recycled denim, Tencel, lace, and sparkle.

Crazy Carding

Crazy carding is the perfect way for spinners, including novice spinners, to make highly unusual and creative yarns easily. The concept is to put as many different colors, textures, and materials as possible into one batt, then spin it into a simple thick-and-thin single. Very little skill is needed on the spinning end, and creating the batt is a fun and liberating exercise.

Crazy carding integrates absolutely any fiber or material that will fit through the carder's drums, including silk waste, felted wool, tinsel, sequins, fabric bits, plant fibers, yarn, sparkle, silk noil, cotton, or anything else you could imagine. Be prepared to push your carder's capabilities to the limit. It is normal for the machine to card very clumpy at first, and it will be hard to crank.

Sandwich formed with bottom layer of wool roving and mohair, fixings in the middle (shredded money, sparkle, thread, blue silk cap, black silk noil, aluminum fibers, and red semifelted wool), and top layer of yellow mohair.

Make a sandwich!

The basic process for crazy carding is to combine several different ingredients at a time and send them through the carder in a thick clump. This will cause the materials to be minimally blended together and will preserve many heavy textures.

Short-fiber materials tend to get caught up in the teeth of the small drum and usually do not make it into the batt. To avoid this, sandwich all the short fibers, or other unusual materials, between layers of longer-stapled fibers such as mohair or processed roving. Visualize making a sandwich: spread a flat layer of mohair or roving out first as the bread, add uncarded locks (lettuce), semifelted wool (tomatoes), sparkle and silk noil (salt and pepper), top with another layer of mohair/roving (bread), and send it through the carder!

Repeat this process adding different fixings in each sandwich. Sandwiches should be about 3" to 4" [7.5 to 10 cm] thick. Card until the large drum is full.

Spin!

Remove the crazy-carded batt from the carder. Starting from the outside edge, pull off spinnable strips and spin a simple thick-and-thin single; do not overdraft. Allow the lumps, bumps, tangles, and textures to remain.

Excerpted from Intertwined.

Tip

Card the batt only once. Over-carded batts tend to lose their interesting textures.

Mini Batts!

Do not discard fibers that are collected on the small drum—this is pure fiber gold! Remove the fiber from the small drum and use this mini batt to add highly textured lumps or nubs to your yarns. This is a great way to make a complement yarn to your crazy-carded single. Spin a single from the big batt, and then spin another yarn in solid-colored roving, adding lumps from the mini-batt to make a coordinated set.

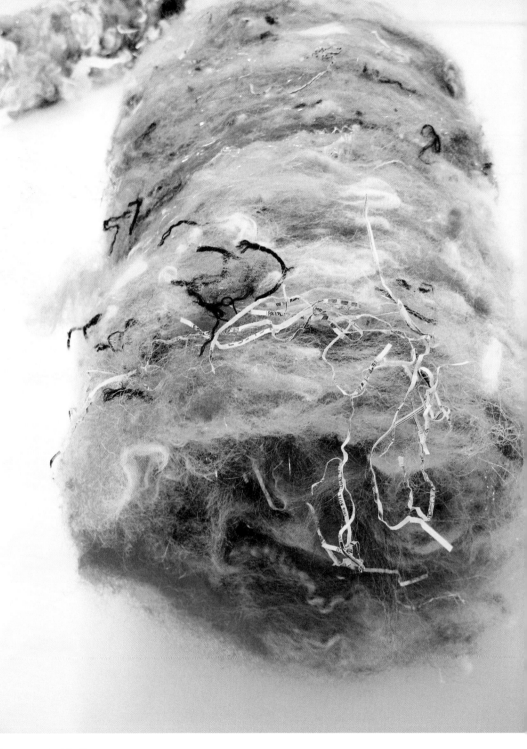

Crazy-carded batt

Stephanie Gorin

Batt and Roving Artist of Loop Fiber
Hudson Valley, New York

It has always been the fiber and fleece that have hooked me into spinning. But I had never fully recognized the creative potential that could be opened through carding—until I saw Stephanie Gorin's batts. I immediately knew what I was looking at: a batt that had crossed the boundary into art. I will never forget the first one I saw years ago; it was ten shades of gold on a background of creamy silk streaked with burnt sienna Tencel. But there is no recounting the colors or sharing of carding techniques to enable replication of that batt. It was a true, spontaneous creation. Her batts are painterly and intuitive, harmonious without signs of control or contrivance. Many of them have attained their highest potential as they are, with no need to make them into something more. Stephanie founded her fiber studio in 2007 under the name Loop and produces her fiber arts in Hudson Valley, NY.

Q and A: Lexi and Stephanie

How did you come to fiber and the arts? Has this been a lifelong pursuit or something unexpected?

My first creative endeavor was ballet. As a kid I was a serious student of dance, on the career track and all that. At 14, scoliosis and a spinal fusion put an end to that dream. As a young adult I turned to creative writing, photography, and theater as creative outlets. None really stuck and I ended up joining the Peace Corps after college. I worked in international development for a decade.

In the midst of building my international development career, someone taught me to knit. I could hardly purl when I put down my knitting needles to search for some interesting yarn for my first project—a scarf. Disappointed with the yarn I found in the many yarn shops, I turned to my computer and eBay to find something more interesting. It was online where

I first encountered handspun and realized I could make my own yarn. I googled spinning instruction, signed up for private lessons, and bought my first spinning wheel. One day my spinning instructor showed me how to use a drum carder to blend fibers. That was the day that changed everything.

It had been over a decade since I'd done anything creative. I'd always admired artists who made something tangible but never seemed to find my medium. When I made my first batt I knew immediately that carding fiber was my thing. Not unlike an addict, I needed to card every day. Within days I'd purchased my first drum carder and a hundred pounds of alpaca fiber. I opened an online fiber business, Loop, where I sold the batts I made. Within a year I quit my job, dropped out of a Ph.D. program, and was running Loop full time. Carding fiber, something I'd never even heard of a year earlier, had completely taken over my life.

What thoughts or feelings did you have the first time you carded a batt?

The first time I made a batt I literally felt euphoric. Carding that first batt was like developing your first photo in a darkroom, but better. As I carded the different colors onto the drum, the batt appeared to me slowly like a photograph. What really hooked me was the drum carder enabled me to play with color in three dimensions. I was just as fascinated with the color effects as I was with the different textures I could create. For me, making batts is an endless experiment and I'm inspired by each discovery I make along the way.

Your batts seem so randomly perfect in their color combinations and selection of fibers. When you're creating a batt are you working consciously?

I do my best work when my mind stays out of it. I'm a pretty analytical person by nature, but for some reason that doesn't work for me creatively. My favorite way to card is spontaneously. What I mean by that is I try not to think while I'm carding. It's an exercise in letting spontaneity take over. I usually card this type of batt loosely so the result is uneven, lumpy, and bumpy in places to create lots of texture and automatic randomness in the hand-spun yarn. I call them Spontaneous Spinning Batts.

Practically speaking, when I card spontaneously, I set up my drum carder on a huge table surrounded by as many fibers in different colors and textures as possible. I card very quickly, and in the process I reach over and grab whatever catches my eye in that instant. I try not to think about how the colors or fibers will combine; I simply stop carding when the drum is full.

Tell us a little about your broader process for producing art batts and spinning fiber. Do you begin with raw fleece? How and where do you gather your materials that finally end up in a batt?

My spinning instructor was old school. She taught me how to process fiber from raw fleece. She taught me how to wash and dye fiber, how to comb and card fiber into different preparations, and how to spin different types of yarn. Unfortunately now that I'm running a full-time business, I don't have time to start from scratch. I especially love dyeing fiber, but don't have time to dye everything I use. Instead I dye the fibers I can't easily find and buy the rest from different suppliers. I try to support independent dyers as much as possible and have developed relationships with several individuals who specialize in processing and dyeing specific fibers.

Platinum Print two-toned batt from 100 percent banana fiber

Spontaneous Spinning Batt from miscellaneous fibers featuring recycled sari silk and sparkle

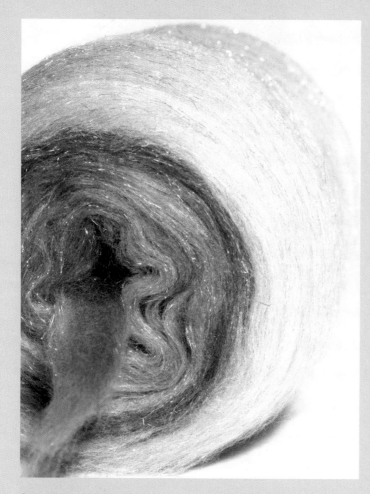

Seaglass, spinning bump

My fiber studio is huge and it's set up like a candy shop with bins of every fiber imaginable and in every possible color. I buy my materials mostly online from other indie fiber artists as well as larger suppliers. I'm always looking for new fabrics and fibers to card. Loop batts are made with every fiber imaginable from soy to yak, to recycled silk and shredded money. The most exciting fiber I've ever carded was from a lion's mane.

Are you thinking about an end use for the batt while you make it—such as specific yarn or felting?

Honestly, no. My creative input ends with my finished product, which is a batt, clouds, or roving. My goal is to make hand-carded batts and hand-spun yarns that are as beautiful as the finished objects produced by those who use them. By focusing on supplies, and not on the end product, I feel like I'm able to share my affinity for fiber with many other crafters. It's my hope that the spontaneous nature of my work will in turn inspire spontaneity in others. Beyond that I don't try to dictate how my customers use my fiber. I expect them to infuse it with their own creativity. This artistic collaboration is what drives my work. Nothing motivates me more than seeing what my customers create with Loop fiber.

Where do you see yourself going in this field? Do you have goals, ideas, or new territories in fiber that you are moving towards?

In 2009 I moved Loop from my fiber-packed living room in Maryland to a 2,500 square foot (232 sq. m) studio in a pre-Civil War textile mill turned arts center in New York's Lower Hudson Valley. The new studio is like a fiber candy store. Visitors can hand pick their favorite color and fiber combinations from the rows of bins and jars lining the shelves. They can blend these ingredients on a drum carder themselves, or have me feed them into my carding machine to make custom clouds or roving. The studio is a perfect setting for fiber gatherings and classes, from carding and spinning to felting and weaving. My dream is for Loop to evolve into a thriving learning-and-teaching community for all kinds of fiber enthusiasts.

Loop spinning batts have appeared on the cover of *Spin-Off* magazine (Winter 2007), and have been featured on the pages of *Spin-Off*, *Craft:* magazine, *Knittyspin*, *DIY City Mag*, *Lime & Violet's Daily Chum*, and numerous spinning websites, blogs, and forums. They are also featured in Sit and Spin, a spinning DVD by Insubordiknit.

above: Spontaneous roving

below: Hard-core yarn by Stephanie Gorin using one of her Spontaneous Spinning Batts

Horse-hair bouclé
plied with black
linen

Chapter 2

Spinning Techniques: Learning vs. Discovery

We learn from others, but we can only discover things by ourselves. It is important and necessary when learning to spin to look at the work that has come before and to practice it. This will lay a good solid foundation of skill. But in order to push your spinning into the creative realm you have to allow yourself to discover things you didn't previously know. How many things have you been taught that you have forgotten? I bet you've lost track. How many things have you figured out how to do on your own that you remember? All of them. There is something in the process of discovery and figuring it out on our own that burns the knowledge into the brain. Curiosity and a drive for discovery happen to be the very foundation of creative thinking. So do yourself a favor, learn a technique or two from this book, and then put it aside for a while. Sit down at your wheel with some fiber and try something new. Ask yourself, "What if?" What if I tangle this up before I spin it? What if I spin in one direction but pull these fibers in a different direction? Who knows, it might not work, it might be a disaster, but it might look good. It doesn't really matter. Being too attached to a preconceived result is the biggest impediment to creativity. There really is no right or wrong way to do something when you are creating. Do not think in terms of failure or success, but rather in the constant build up of knowledge. It doesn't matter how it turns out, what matters is now you know how it turns out, and why.

Treasure

We all have that one drawer, tub, bag, or hamper that tends to collect all sorts of fiber odds and ends. You know the one, it has the stuff you scraped off the drum carder, or the remains of some roving you didn't spin through. And you've dug through it so many times that half of it has started to felt and all the colors are mixed up. What a mess, right? Wrong! What you actually have is a veritable treasure trove of spontaneous, wonderful, surprising little bits of fiber stuck together in forms and combinations you could never have come up with consciously. Next time you pull that drawer open, pull it all the way out, and dump the contents on the floor. Spend a little time mining through this eclectic collection and pull out any little bits that catch your eye. Don't worry if they don't match or whether there is a common theme. The idea here is to appreciate each incidence of fiber for what it is, in and of itself, like gems among stones.

Fiber Prep

Glean a nice collection of treasures from your random fiber stash and set them aside. Choose any fiber you like for the basis of this yarn. If you are thinking of using commercial combed-top, consider running it through the carder first with about 10 percent noncommercial fiber. This will make it easier to add the treasures into the fiber. (Combed top can be dense and resistant to adding things in.)

Spin!

Begin spinning a single as you normally would using the fiber you chose as your base material. When you are ready to add in a treasure, draft a thin spot (thin spots attract more twist) in the roving you are spinning, lay an edge of the treasure in, and then allow the treasure to wrap in from the side. As the twist

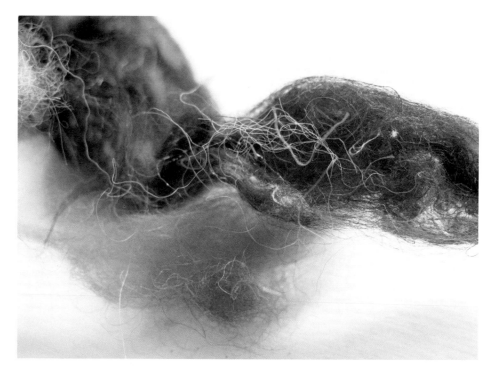

Treasure = beautiful, intriguing, and serendipitous instances of fiber juxtaposition.

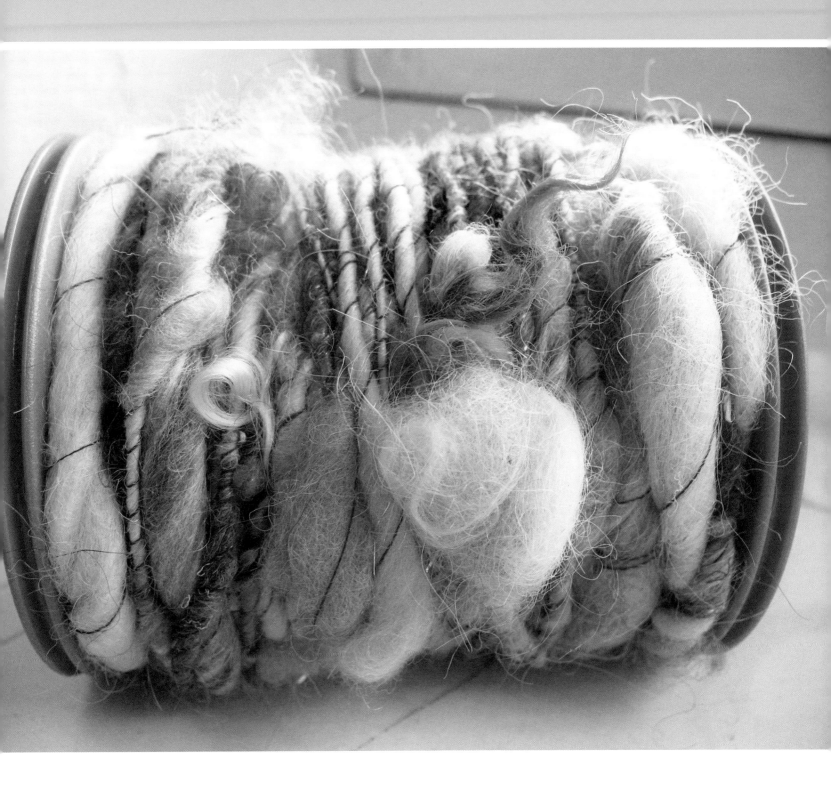

Miscellaneous stash of fiber—a gold mine!

sure to show it off. If it's not showing, try spinning slow and loose when you add the treasure in, taking only the ends in and leaving the treasure slightly un-spun.) Spin until all your treasures are in the yarn. It's best to make an assessment ahead of time as to how much space to spin between each treasure in order to give you enough final yardage.

Note: When you are adding in a treasure, you are essentially core spinning. One thing is wrapping around the yarn in the center. Please review and practice the core-spinning techniques on page 64 if you are having any difficulty adding in your special fibers.

Set the Twist
Soak the spun yarn in hot water and set to dry with tension if it is over-twisted.

runs through the treasure, be sure and bring the treasure's fibers into the base fibers so they twist together. If the treasure piece is long in shape, you may need to break off the base roving, attach the treasure, spin through it, reattach the base roving, and continue from there.

Pay close attention to each individual treasure. Identify the parts of each piece that are your favorites and do your best to make sure those elements don't get hidden in the twist. (For example, a pretty little strand that dangles nicely or a certain pink spot. Whatever it is that makes it special, be

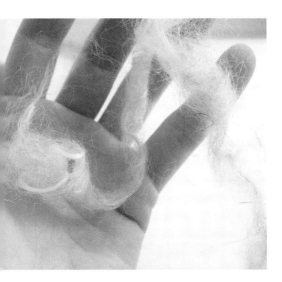

Look for the little nuances that make each bit interesting.

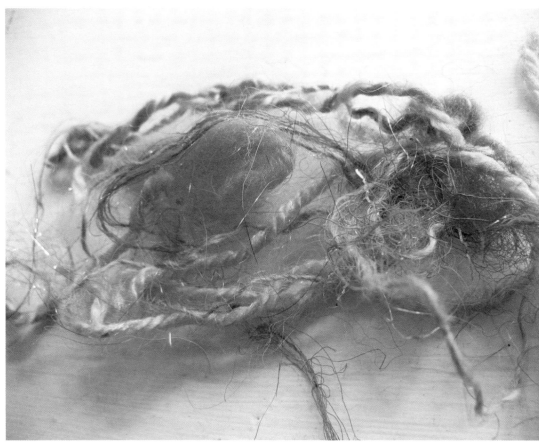

Don't weed out the occasional thread, yarn, or fabric. Who knows what might end up in the treasure trove? I found a furry tail once, and yes, I spun it.

Twists

Lavender merino carded with black silk noil, spun thick and thin, and plied with silk thread by Pluckyfluff.

Materials
4 oz [113 g] fiber of choice
100 yds [91.5 cm] plying thread

Wool works best for this technique, but almost any fiber can be made to work. Use a fiber that has a lot of memory and tends to hold its twist. These twists can also be added strategically. For example, you can spin a yarn with mohair and every now and then add a 3" to 4" (7.5 to 10 cm) section of wool. When you ply the yarns, the wool will twist but the mohair will stay relatively straight.

You can do this with wool and silk, wool and hemp, wool and cotton, and so forth. In an all-wool yarn it will be the thin sections that make the twists and the thick sections that remain straight. So if you are going to use 100 percent wool, you must spin it thick and thin! The following instructions are for an all-wool yarn.

Fiber Prep
Select some wool for the yarn. Hand-carded or lightly processed wool is best as it retains the most energy and loft. Superwash, combed top, and other over-processed wools can be pretty dead and will require a lot more twist to get the life back into them.

Next, decide how you want this yarn to look. If you want the twists to be subtle, then choose one color scheme for the entire yarn. However, if you want the twists to contrast, then choose a different color for the twists. Break the twist's roving into small pieces, just enough to spin into 3" to 4" (7.5 to 10 cm) long sections. Prepare the remaining wool by splitting it into easy-to-spin sections.

Spin!
Begin spinning a simple single. Be sure to spin a thick-and-thin yarn. An evenly spun yarn will not twist as easily! If you are spinning a single color scheme, simply spin through the fiber. If making contrasting twists, spin the base color

then every few yards [meters], or as often as you like, stop and spin in a small 3" to 4" (7.5 to 10 cm) section in the contrasting color. Spin through the fiber, remove bobbin, and prepare to ply.

Ply!

Select a delicate yet strong thread to ply with. Attach your wool single and plying thread to the leader string and begin to spin in the opposite direction that you spun the single in. Keep more tension on the thread, and less on the single. Keep the thread directly in front of you and let the single wind on at a 45-degree angle. Ply in this manner for a few yards (meters). If you are spinning a solid color, simply watch the single as it approaches your hands; it will have spots where it is naturally twisted. Take advantage of these places. As the twist approaches, grab it with one hand, pinching the base of the twist so it does not straighten out. With the other hand, guide the ply down to the upcoming twist. Ply right up to the base of the twist, keeping it pinched the whole time. Tightly ply past the base of the twist and on through the single. Repeat for every twist that approaches.

For contrasting twists, work this process for every twist-color section that approaches. If the section does not want to twist naturally, twist it by hand and follow the steps described previously.

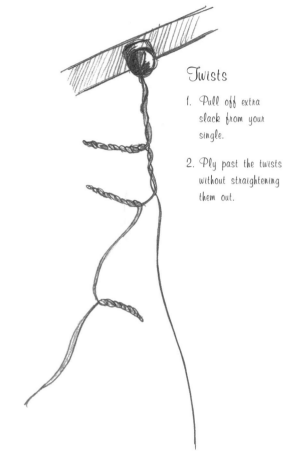

Twists

1. Pull off extra slack from your single.

2. Ply past the twists without straightening them out.

Set the Twist

Unwind the bobbin onto a niddy noddy. Make a hot water bath and remove the skein from the niddy noddy. Soak the skein for ten to twenty minutes. Place the skein in the washing machine, set on spin cycle, and spin to remove excess water. Hang the skein to dry.

Excerpted from Intertwined

Twist on "Twists"

Michelle Snowdon,
Wooldancer Yarn Designs
Australia

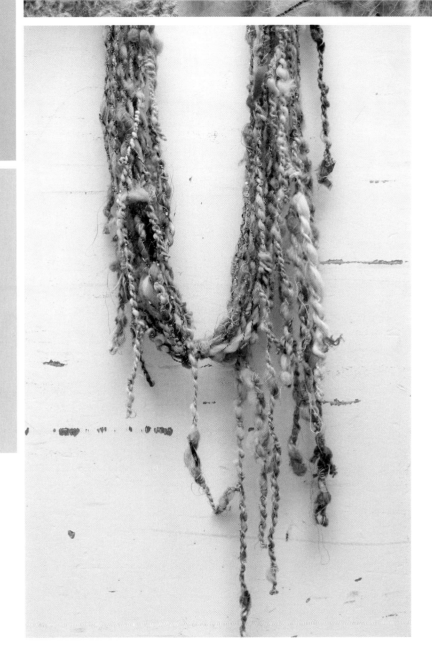

Take twists to an extreme with this dramatic technique from Michelle Snowdon. Follow the instructions for "Twists" but when you want to make a twist, pull an arms-length of slack off the bobbin, double it over and pinch it at the base against the plying thread. Let this big loop twist around itself. Reconnect the plying thread to the remaining single coming off the bobbin and continue plying as usual. You can vary the lengths of these twists as you like. Sometimes the loop will form a few twists in one, this looks good too!

Note: Depending on your orifice and hooks, you may have to hand wind the big twists onto the bobbin.

opposite page: This yarn hangs so nicely as is—it's a perfect candidate for an un-knit scarf! Michelle Snowdon

Twisted

Here's a deceptively simple technique to get a really exaggerated effect. This ultra shaggy yarn is perfect for trims and accents or knit it densely for a bathmat or house slippers! The plying stage of this technique really eats the yardage, so be sure and spin at least five times the length you want to end up with.

Equipment
This yarn requires a wheel with a large orifice and preferably enclosed guides. The loops and twists tend to get hung up quite easily on regular hooks and pegs.

Materials
Any fiber for the single
Very strong plying material (try heavy commercial mohair yarn)

Note: Make sure you use a plying material that is at least a two-ply. This technique would simply untwist (or over twist) a single ply yarn.

Spin!
Drink two double cappucino's and a Red Bull and begin spinning your fiber of choice into a simple single—but here's the trick—severely over-twist it. I don't mean just a little active twist, I

mean spin it until it coils up all over itself when you give it some slack. To do this, spin a length, and then hold it back from feeding onto the bobbin while you treadle for a few extra moments. To test if there is enough twist, stop treadling, and relax the yarn. See if it forms a mass of tangled twists; if so, you're good to go. Continue spinning until you have a full bobbin.

Ply!

Start with an empty bobbin. To make this yarn shaggy you're going to ply it by the handfuls. Normally when you ply, you're bringing the two plies together nice and evenly. For this one, do the extreme opposite! Get your strong plying material, such as commercial mohair yarn or some other strong (but not too thick) yarn, and attach it to your leader along with your over-spun single. Ply normally for a while to get started and to give yourself a section of yarn to tie off with later. When you're ready to make it shaggy, reach down and pull a yard or so of single off the bobbin. Pile this into your lap, making sure there is lots of slack. Pull extra yarn off so you have a fair amount of twists to work with. Grab this twisted yarn by the handfuls and ply through it making sure that lots of twists and tangles remain. It is helpful to keep all the tension on the plying material and align it directly between you and the orifice. You'll be piling on the tangles from the side. Once you've plied through a few inches (centimeters) be sure to wind it onto the bobbin. Techniques like these tend to put a lot of twist into the core yarn and it can snap it if gets too much. Feeding the yarn onto the bobbin regularly is very important and will help avoid the breakage.

Once you've plied through the whole bobbin, ply the last few inches [centimeters] normally for a length of yarn to tie off with.

Set the Twist

Soak the yarn in hot water, and then dry with a bit of tension if it's overtwisted. (Really, no pun intended! You may have a lot of twists, but it's possible to spin this yarn so that the skein hangs balanced.)

Elastic Twist

The following is a refined technique by Flore Vallery-Radot of Tricotin.com, Paris, France. The result is an elastic yarn achieved by over-twisting singles, and then plying them together. This technique requires some extra preparation and focus, but is well worth the effort!

opposite page: This style can be bulky enough to make an easy and dramatic trim.

right: Twisted Shag Elastika by Flore Vallery-Radot

Materials
Combed or carded roving

Fiber Prep
Before you begin, strip the roving down to arm-length sections about as thick as your finger. Make sure the roving is not too compacted. If it seems stiff or difficult to draft, loosen it up by pulling on it and predrafting it a bit. The goal is to get the strips to be as even and equal to each other in width as possible. Assemble these strips in a place where you can easily reach them.

Make sure the roving is predrafted and separated into even, usable strips.

Yarn coiling on itself due to over-spinning

Spin!

Begin spinning a single as you normally would. After a few inches (centimeters) pull back on the yarn to keep it from feeding into the orifice, but keep treadling! As you treadle the yarn will begin to kink up and coil around itself. As it does this, slowly guide the twist into the strip of roving. Be sure and go slow enough that you can control each kink and make it line up right behind the previous one. If you spin too quickly, the kink can get reversed and there's no way to undo that glitch. Spin through half of your fiber in this manner. Change the bobbin, and then spin the rest of the fiber onto the second bobbin.

Ply!

Ply these two over-twisted singles together in the opposite direction than they were spun. The singles may be bumpy, but they'll ply just like any other single would.

If spun bulky, this yarn can be heavy and stiff. Start thin for a more flexible yarn.

Tail

A quick and easy way to tail spin without bothering with a core material, is to simply spin uncarded locks of wool or mohair together making an effort to let the tips of the locks stick out. This is a step up from spinning plain uncarded fiber except here you need to be cognizant of the tips as you go.

Materials
Uncarded wool or mohair locks (Any breed will work if it has distinct tips.)

Fiber Prep
Do not card these fibers. Simply pull them apart if they are in big clumps and gently tease the fibers from the base end of the locks out a bit. The idea here is to get the fiber from the base end nice and fluffy so you can spin it easily. Refrain from touching the tips too much; you want them to remain intact.

Spin!
Spin your fiber in a normal manner long enough to get your yarn started on the bobbin. When you're ready to tail spin, pick up a very small handful of locks (two or three) and attach them to the spinning yarn by adding the fluffed-up base section first. Now, concentrate on guiding the twist down through the fluffy parts only, twisting and joining them together while simultaneously skipping over the tips when they come along. It sounds more difficult than it is, so don't over think the process, just grab a small handful and get started. Make sure you have ample enough take-up to pull the shaggy yarn onto the bobbin. Continue spinning through your fiber in this manner, drafting through the base sections, and skipping over the tips.

Note: If the tips seem to get caught in the twist, simply pause a moment to gently pull them out. This is normal and may take a little extra effort to make sure they really show!

Tail spinning

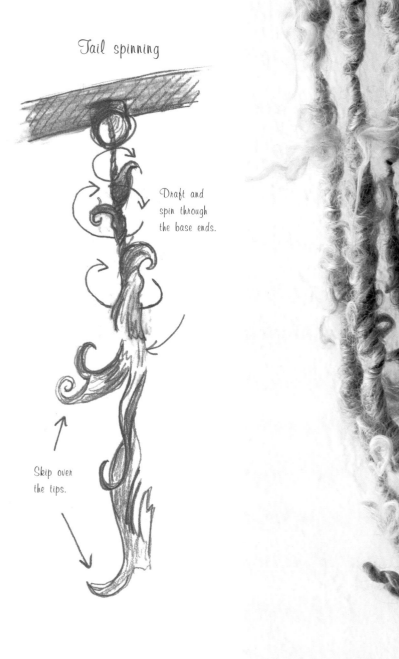

Draft and spin through the base ends.

Skip over the tips.

Tail-spun yarn by Natasha Marquez Sills

Falling

This is a fun variation on tail spinning sent to me by Natalie Redding of Namaste Farms, who raises Angora goats with incredibly long locks. She has found this technique to be an easy way to retain the natural quality of the pretty, uncarded mohair locks. Try this technique with mohair or any other exceptionally long locks.

Materials

Uncarded locks (Look for long, lustrous, eye-catching locks for this yarn!)

Thread or lace-weight yarn for plying

Fiber Prep

Take a look at your locks to see if they are connected together in clumps or if they are already in individual locks. If they are connected a bit at the base, then take a little time to separate them and lay all the locks out on a worksurface or in a grab bag.

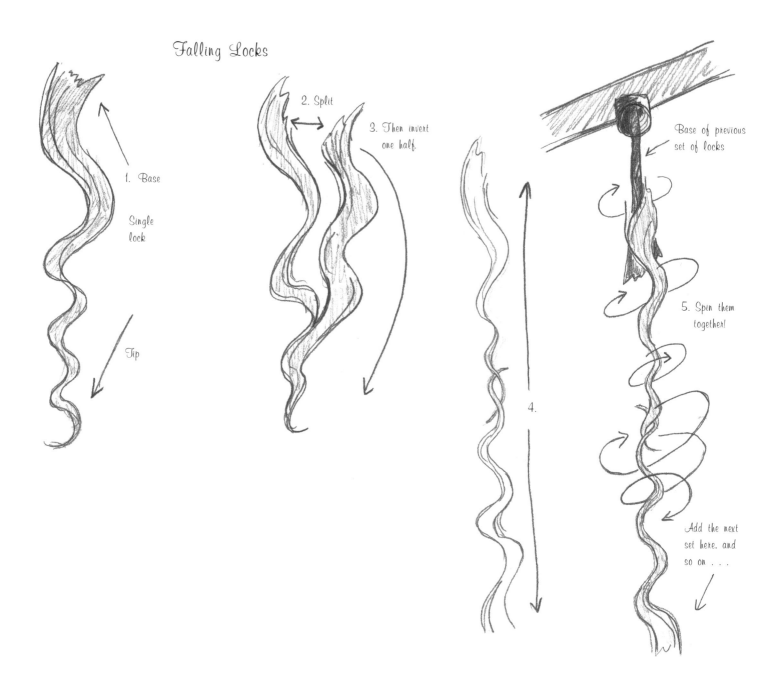

Falling Locks

1. Base

Single lock

Tip

2. Split

3. Then invert one half.

4.

Base of previous set of locks

5. Spin them together!

Add the next set here. and so on . . .

Spin!

To make the single, start with a bit of carded mohair to get your yarn started. Once you've spun a short bit, start adding the locks. Taking a lock at a time, hold it by the base with the tip dangling down. Split the lock in half starting at the base end. Pull it apart most of the way but keep the tip part intertwined. Let the newly separated half hang down, doubling the length of the lock. To add this fiber into your yarn, simply attach one base end to the fiber you are spinning, guide the twist through the set of locks, leaving a bit unspun at the end. To this end add the next split-lock piece. Continue in this manner until the bobbin is full.

Note: You can emphasize the curly tips by pulling them out a bit as you spin past them.

Ply!

The idea behind using a thin yarn or thread to ply is that it will re-create the waviness of the original lock without giving the yarn added bulk. Try using a thread similar in color to the fiber to disguise the fact that the yarn is plied and not just one long curly lock!

Extreme Tail Spin

Long Teeswater locks are perfect for dramatic tail spinning.

Materials

4 oz (113 g) uncarded long staple locks
Quill or large orifice spinning wheel
Sturdy core material (Try strong, commercial mohair.)

Fiber Prep

Separate locks into 1" to 3"-wide (2.5 to 7.5 cm) groups. Identify the base and the tip of each group of locks and arrange them so all of the locks are orientated in the same direction. You will be spinning the base of the locks onto the core material.

Spin!

Thread the core material through the leader string, and using regular wool roving, spin a simple single for 10" to 12" (25.5 to 30.5 cm). Begin adding the uncarded locks. Using one or two locks at a time, lay the base of the locks (the end that was sheared, not the narrow tip) against the core material at a 90-degree angle. Spin, using your thumb and forefinger to pinch and guide the base fiber of the lock as it twists onto the core material. Spin slowly and be sure to attach only the base of the lock, allowing the tips to

Extreme tail-spun yarn by Esther Rodgers of Jazzturtle Creations

Extreme Tail Spinning

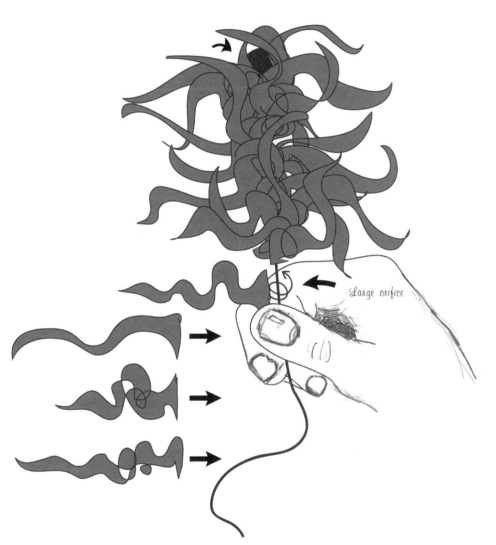

Large orifice

hang free. Once a lock is attached, stop the wheel keeping the base of that lock pinched, and then grab the next group of uncarded locks, and repeat.

Note: Be sure to work close to the orifice at all times. As you spin, twist is building up in the core material and if over-twist it could break. If you are spinning back into your lap you are probably building up too much twist. Spin a few inches (centimeters) at a time, then stop and wind it onto the bobbin. Think of this technique as yarn building, rather than yarn spinning.

This technique is a very slow process. You will be starting and stopping every couple of inches (5 cm). Proceed until all the fiber is spun or until the bobbin is full. After the final lock is attached, tack on some wool roving, and spin 10" to 12" (25.5 to 30.5 cm) as a simple single (to be used for tying off the skein).

Unwind the yarn onto a niddy noddy, and use the spun-single sections to tie off. A full bobbin may provide you with only 3 to 4 yards (2.75 to 3. 65 m) of yarn.

Excerpted from Intertwined

In-Line Crochet

Why wait until the yarn is done to crochet it? Keep a crochet hook handy when you are spinning to easily add interesting designs while you spin!

Materials
Any fiber
Crochet hook

Spin!
Begin spinning a simple single as you normally would. When you want to add some crochet, break off the roving you're spinning from, and wind the single around one hand, backing the yarn off the bobbin. Back out as much yarn as you need in order to crochet whatever you want. To begin the chain, make a loop in the yarn near the orifice and knot it—you have your first stitch. Crochet from there, working from the yarn wound around your hand. When you have crocheted all the yarn, pull the end through the last loop to fasten off. Wind the crochet on the bobbin, reconnect the roving to the end of the single, and continue spinning.

Heather Baris-Lightbody (of Girl with a Hook) helping to work out this technique

A simple single chain adds a lot of character.

In-Line Add-ins

The following is a technique for adding linear items into your yarn so they stay in line with the yarn, becoming part of the strand as opposed to wrapping around it. This is a good way to include things such as chain, strung beads, lace, zippers, trims, etc. You can add anything that is arranged in a linear fashion.

Materials

Look for linear items that you would like to have in your yarn and that can be presented in its straight form. Things that already have a closed loop or ring at each end are best (such as the last ring on a chain). If the item does not have something like this, fear not, you can always slip a ring on the end. If you use fabric, you can cut a hole at each end.

Fiber Prep

Just about any fiber will do for this project, so go with what inspires you. However, while learning the technique, steer clear of extremely short fibers such as cotton or down. Have your roving or batt arranged and ready to go.

Prepare the Add-ins!

Whatever the item is, it should have some way to loop a yarn through each end. If it is a necklace, remove the clasp but leave a ring at each end. If it is a fabric-based item, such as zippers or

Yarn with chains by Ashley Martineau of Neauveau Fiber Arts

Hint

Before you begin, make sure the linear items you select will fit through the orifice!

trims, use scissors to cut a small hole in each end. If you have strings of beads with no connectors, try tying a metal jump ring at each end. If the beads are on a strong string, tie a loop in that.

Spin!

Begin spinning your fiber by making a basic single ply. When you are ready to add in your item, stop treadling, break off your roving, and leave a few inches (centimeters) unspun. Thread the roving through the ring or loop on your item, and then double it back onto itself. Tuck the end fibers up into the unspun roving to make sure they will integrate; keep the fiber pinched together at this connection. Begin treadling and guide the twist through this double-backed section of roving until it twists up tight against the loop or ring of your item.

Stop treadling at this point; you don't want to put a bunch of twist into your add-in. Hand wind the section with the add-in onto the bobbin until just the very end is sticking out. Get some more fiber or roving, thread it through the ring/loop of your item and double it back into itself. Keep that connection pinched under your fingers and begin treadling, guiding the twist through the join. Let the rest of the item wind onto the bobbin, and continue spinning your fiber as usual.

Repeat this process for each remaining item.

Set the twist!

Since you cannot ply this yarn (well ... you could, I suppose, but it would be a whole different thing—try it next time) you will want to set the twist by soaking it in hot water for twenty minutes. Spin out the excess water in the washing machine and let dry with some tension on it.

In-Line Braids

This lovely technique was developed by Tove Skolseg of Lillehammer, Norway, and is a great use for balls of roving that manage to get somewhat felted in the bottom of your stash—you know the ones—it takes major effort just to split them in two. For this project, you will need to split them into three sections and use them to make a braid in your yarn. Since they are partially felted, they will have enough integrity to stay together in your yarn without any twist.

Use the same or different colors of roving to achieve different effects.

Materials
Semifelted roving or other roving, which will hold together on it's own fairly well.

Fiber Prep
Prepare a batt, or choose some roving to be the base material for your yarn. This will be the part you spin normally and will serve as a backdrop to the braids. Choose something that will readily join with the roving you chose for the braids. To learn, I suggest sticking with wool or mohair blends. Branch out once you get the hang of it!

Prepare the felted roving by tearing them into lengths, and then tear each length into three strips. Braid the three strips together, being careful to leave a few inches [centimeters] of fiber unbraided at each end. Take some time to draft out the braid ends, loosening up the fibers as much as possible because otherwise they will be spun into your yarn. (To accentuate the braid, roll each strip between your hands before braiding, making them even more felted.) Lay the braids out in your workspace so they are handy.

Spin!
Begin spinning a basic single with your batt or roving. When you are ready to add a braid, break off the roving you are working with leaving a few inches of unspun fiber at the end. Pick up the braid and lay one end of it into the fiber you are spinning. Be sure to integrate the fibers from the braid into the fibers

Braided yarn by Tove Skolseg

of your single, pinch them together at the join, and begin treadling again. Guide the twist through the join until the braid is tightly attached to your yarn.

Don't twist the braid! Once it's joined, stop treadling and hand wind the entire length of the braid onto the bobbin until the tail end of it is sticking out of the orifice. Fluff apart the fibers at the end of the braid, pick up some more roving or batt and lay its fibers within the braid end. Keeping the join pinched together, begin treadling again guiding the twist through the end of the braid into the roving. Once joined, wind it onto the bobbin and continue spinning your fiber like normal.

Repeat for each braid.

Set the Twist

Soak the yarn in hot water for twenty minutes. Spin out excess water in a top-loading washing machine and set the yarn to dry with tension. If braids seem twisted, go through and untwist them while the yarn is still wet.

Quick Coils!

This is a newer, quicker version of my old technique "Supercoils" (*Intertwined*, Quarry Books, 2008). With a little tricky hand positioning you can easily ply your single into this very coily yarn.

Materials

A prespun single (A little over-twist in the single will prove helpful for this technique.)

Plying material: something strong with two or more plies

Ply!

On your wheel set the twist to low (drive band on the biggest whorl). Attach the single and the plying thread/yarn to the leader. Spin in the opposite direction than when you spun the single. Ply normally for a few inches (centimeters) to give yourself a length of yarn to tie the skein off with when you're done. Make sure the tension is strong, as this lumpy yarn can get sluggish through the orifice.

Now, hold the single in your drafting hand and let it run through your fingers right up against the plying thread.

Hold the plying thread in the other hand, controlling the speed it travels through by keeping it against your palm with your last three fingers. Using the index finger of this hand, apply strong downward pressure on the plying thread. From your view, the single and the ply should appear intersecting head-on. If you draw an invisible line between your belly and the orifice, both plies should be intersecting the line at a 90-degree angle. Your single should be coming on without much tension while the plying material has a lot of tension from your index finger. Your drafting hand should be delivering the single just above the fingernail of this pressure finger. As the single wraps around in horizontal coils, allow the plying thread to wind onto the bobbin at an equal rate.

Once you've plied through your bobbin, be sure to spin the last few inches (centimeters) normally to give yourself something to tie off with.

Set the Twist
Soak the yarn in hot water, spin excess water out in a top-loading washing machine, and hang to dry. If the yarn is over-twisted, hang with a little weight.

Notice the downward pressure being applied to the plying thread on the right. The other hand is simply guiding the single so it stacks up in neat coils.

Note: Spinning is not a handed activity. Just because I use my right or left hand for things doesn't mean that will work for you. If it feels awkward, try switching hands.

Variation

Quick Coil Thick-and-Thin

Try this same technique with a thick-and-thin single for dramatic results. It works well with gradual slubs, or try spinning a single with the occasional dense lumpy bit. Experiment and see what happens!

left to right: Thick-and-thin Navaho ply, Navaho-plied quick-coiled coreless core-spun (That's what I said!), and coreless core-spun

Chapter 3

New Twists: Expanding Traditional Techniques

I n this section we will look at three traditional techniques—core spinning, Navaho plying, and spinning raw fiber—and explore what happens when they are pushed beyond their conventional boundaries. These are all methods that have been around for a long time, and we will see some examples of how exaggerating the inherent properties of a well-honed form can produce very surprising results. It is imperative to first master these basic techniques in their traditional forms, which were quite inventive for their time (even if that was 15,000 years ago). A lot can be learned from walking a few miles in the deerskin slippers of our ancestors. Most important, you gain an appreciation of what the technique was intended to look like and how it was meant to function. This creates a solid foundation on which you can build, compare, contrast, deconstruct, or do a two-step across. It's important to start at the beginning, but to realize you don't have to stay there.

Core Spinning: Basic

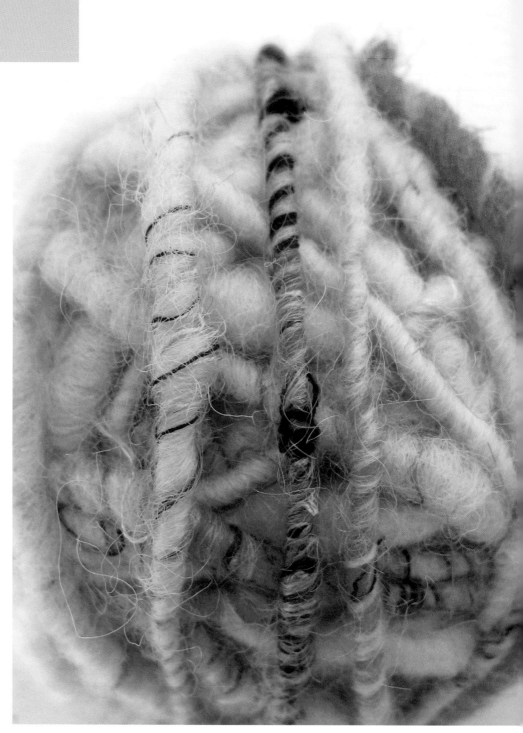

The earliest known examples of core spinning are cotton embroidery threads that date back to 3,000 B.C. in England. Core spinning historically had functional advantages such as added strength and durability. Yarns spun on a core with a bit of air between the core and the sheath have enhanced insulating properties, and result in warmer materials. The very basic definition of a core-spun yarn is that it's a two-component yarn with a core and a sheath. Historically these components were made from traditional materials such as cotton or wool. But in theory, if your only constraint is that it be two components, one material wrapped around another, well . . . the sky's the limit.

Materials

When learning to core spin it is important to use fibers that are not overly processed, stuck together, dense, or too slippery. That weeds out most commercial combed-top rovings, superwash wool, pure silk, or other slippery rov-

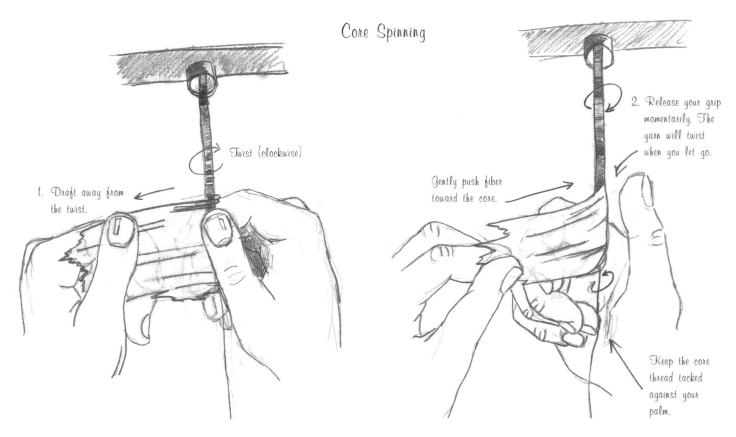

Core Spinning

1. Draft away from the twist.

Twist (clockwise)

Gently push fiber toward the core.

2. Release your grip momentarily. The yarn will twist when you let go.

Keep the core thread tacked against your palm.

ings such as corn silk. It is possible to core spin with these rovings, however it is very difficult to learn to use them in the form they were purchased. Your best bet is to run these fibers through a drum carder with some less processed fibers. Over-processed fibers tend to be lifeless and have less grab. You want something that will readily attach itself to your core material. Card your fibers nice and fine; if you have a lumpy, bumpy batt, spinning it will be more difficult. (Once you get the hang of core spinning, try a more textured batt and see what it does!)

Fiber Prep
Card a nice lofty batt with a small percentage of long stapled, grabby fiber (such as mohair).

Choose a Core!
The material for your core should be a commercially produced yarn or fine string. Make sure it's thin but strong and at least two ply. DO NOT use a single ply (handspun or commercial) as your core. If you spin in the opposite direction it was spun, it will unravel and break. If you spin in the same direction,

it will be over-twisted. (Over-twist is inherent in core-spun yarns already, so we try not to exacerbate it!) In my opinion commercial mohair yarn is ideal as a core material. It has its own re-enforced core threads, the mohair fibers are long and grabby, and want to bond with something! This makes it easy to get your fiber to wrap onto the core.

Spin!
Attach the core material and some fiber to your leader, and then spin normally for a few inches (centimeters) to get

Hard-core yarn by Stephanie Gorin of Loop Fiber

started. When you're ready, peel off a thin, short strip from your batt. It is best to work with little bits of fiber at a time when you're learning. The less you have in your hand the less you will have to jumble up!

Take a minute to think about how you normally draft. Usually you guide the twist with one hand while you draft the fibers towards your belly, right? Right! Now you'll have to retrain your brain in terms of drafting. Drafting is an unconscious movement for most of us, and this will be the biggest hurdle to overcome.

So take a deep breath, then maybe a swig of whiskey, and picture yourself doing this: Hold the core material and guide the twist with one hand, while at the same time drafting away from it (with your drafting hand) at a 90-degree angle from the core material. Yes it's true! You are drafting to the side, per-pendicular to the yarn you are spinning. How does that work, you say? It works like this: The core material is spinning to the right as it rotates, the fibers from the mohair core grab onto the fibers from your batt, and try to carry them along. If the fibers from your batt are fed on at a 90-degree angle they will wrap AROUND the core instead of along with it as in normal spinning.

Now here's the trick. Getting the fiber to begin wrapping around the core is easy. Keeping it going is more difficult. Use the hand that is holding

the core material to gently pinch fibers from the batt you are holding. At the same time draft the fibers away from the core—this is how you control the thickness of the yarn you are spin-ning. After you pinch and draft, briefly release your hold on the core material. This will cause it to rotate quickly and wrap all the drafted fiber around itself. After a couple rotations, grab it again to stop the twist, pinch more fibers out, draft, and release. Keep repeating this sequence as you move along. It's best to work close to the orifice and allow the yarn to feed onto the bobbin as soon as possible. If you spin back into your lap you will build up way too much twist. Take advantage of the pull created by the core material tugging at the fibers.

If you draft away from the rotation of the core, it will help to thin the fibers out as you spin.

Note: The majority of the fiber should be wrapping on above the hand that is hold-ing the core! Be sure that this wrapping action is happening in the space between your hand and the orifice, not between your hand and yourself.

Set the Twist

Core-spun yarns are over-twisted; that's just a fact. Soak the yarn in very hot water for 20 minutes, and then place in a top-loading washing machine set on the spin cycle to remove excess water. Hang to dry with a weight, or stretch between chairs to dry.

Core Spinning: Fluffy!

You can apply the same basic concept of core spinning to different materials and get diverse effects. By teasing the fibers out dramatically while core spinning you can get a very furry, fluffy core-spun yarn.

Start with lofty, fluffy fibers and you can't go wrong!

Materials
Any fiber except silky, smooth fibers, sturdy core, at least two-ply

Fiber Prep
Make a furry yarn from just about any fiber by carding a fluffy, airy batt! Fluff is the key here, so steer clear of silky smooth fibers such as banana, silk, nylon, etc. Run your mix of fibers through the carder once or twice and you're ready to go! Chose a sturdy commercial material for the core that is at least a two-ply—commercial mohair yarn works great.

Spin!
Attach the core material and some fiber from your batt to the leader and spin normally for a few inches [centimeters]. Now, using the core-spinning technique, begin drafting the fiber away from the core at a 90-degree angle, and then allow it wrap back on from the side at 90-degrees. To make it fluffy, draft more vigorously! Pull the fiber almost off the core before allowing it to wrap back on. Use your other hand to pinch the fiber back onto the core in-between drafts. DO NOT use your hand to smooth down the yarn before it goes into the orifice! Once you have drafted it into fluffiness, let it go! Don't touch it! (This is another ingrained motion that requires major brain override. In normal spinning you draft first, then use your other hand to smooth it down.

Fluffy core spinning is the opposite: You pinch the fiber against the core, draft it out, and then throw it back around the core between your hand and the orifice; don't smooth it! Don't worry, you'll get it, just be sure you're not chewing gum while you try.)

Set the Twist
Soak it in hot water for twenty minutes, spin out excess water in a top-loading washing machine, and hang with tension to dry.

Core Spinning: Mohairy

Carding

Lay the mohair out in a thin layer on the bed of the drum carder or hand carders. On top of the mohair make another thin layer of sparkle and little bits of colorful wool or other fiber that is not weighty, such as silk noil or little threads. Lay another layer of mohair on top of this, sandwiching the sparkle in between the mohair. Run this through the carder (or hand card). Repeat the process with the remaining materials.

Core material

Choose a yarn that will look interesting when seen through the mohair. Pompoms, bright colors, or metallic threads or fibers work very well, but almost any novelty yarn will be attractive. Don't use bulky yarns for the core, mid- to light-weight yarns work best.

Materials

2 oz (56.5 g) mohair clouds (see resources, page 158)

100 yds (91.5 m) novelty yarn with decorative elements such as pom-poms, or bright colors that will show well

¼ oz (7 g) sparkle or silk noil (optional)

Fiber Prep

The key to achieving this look is to start with the right mohair. Do not use fine combed, densely packed mohair roving. The roving should be in cloud form: either light, airy rolags, or hand/drum carded batts. The mohair should be light, fluffy, and translucent.

Tip

Beginners should choose a core thread with a rough texture so the mohair will grab on more readily. Commercial mohair yarn is an easy one to start with.

Spin!

Attach the core thread and some mohair to the leader string on your bobbin. Begin spinning normally to get the wheel started. Spin a few feet (1 m) to make sure everything is working properly. Once the yarn is on the bobbin, reduce the tension until there is very little pull into the orifice. If your tension is too tight it will pull the yarn out of your hand before you can get it fluffy enough.

While spinning, hold the core thread and a small amount of mohair in one hand, and use your other hand to tease the majority of the mohair out and pile it back on itself. As the core thread twists, it will grab onto the very loose mohair fibers. Let the fibers twist around the core just enough to coat it very lightly. If it begins to twist too densely, tease the fiber back out in that spot. The handwork here is tricky; one hand should always hold the core thread, but it takes both hands to simultaneously tease the fiber around the core.

As soon as the mohair is laid on in a sheer wrap, allow that section to wind onto the bobbin. Repeat this process with the remainder of your fiber.

Set the Twist

This yarn should be pretty balanced without being set, but it is still a good idea to make it perfectly straight. Soak the skein in hot water for three to five minutes, transfer to washing machine, set machine on spin cycle, and spin until excess water is removed. Remove the skein and give it a good shake to fluff out the fibers. Hang or lay flat to dry with no tension. The yarn will lose its loftiness if you stretch it during the drying process. This yarn should virtually float when it's dry!

Note: If you're a beginner, your first attempts at this technique may yield an over-twisted yarn. If so, you will need to put more tension on your skein while it dries. Use a yarn tensioner, or strand the skein between two chairs.

Excerpted from Intertwined

Tip

Don't wait for the core thread to pull the mohair on, as the twist is too delicate to detect. Instead, push the mohair onto the core as it is twisting.

Core Spinning: Coreless

Yes that's what I said! Spinning a core-spun yarn without a core material. For this yarn we are going to form a core from the same fiber you are spinning, simultaneously wrapping the fiber around it.

Picture this: You are working with a small handful of fiber that is fanned out thin as it comes out of the orifice. Imagine leading more twist into the inside edge of the fiber while drafting the outside edge away from it at a 90-degree angle. Whatever fiber is directly in-line between you and the orifice is going to get the twist. So keep a thin strand of fibers along this line at all times while using your other hand to pull the remaining fibers out of the twist zone.

Draft at a 90-degree angle at all times! Note how thin this fiber has been drafted to begin with and how little fiber I'm holding. The more fiber you have in your hand, the more fiber you can mess up trying to get the hang of it. So do yourself a favor and work with airy, small handfuls.

Fiber Prep

To learn this technique, don't confuse yourself by using a bunch of different fibers. Try something fairly uniform but not over processed. A small farm produced roving that is fairly airy is your best bet. If the roving is too dense, thick, spongy, or processed, the spinning will be more difficult. If the roving doesn't look airy enough, run it through a drum carder. Working from batts is also a good option.

Practice First

Can you spin one-handed? Peel off a very thin strip of roving, pencil-size if you can. Begin spinning normally, then put your drafting hand away. Draw the twist through the fiber with your other hand, allowing it to twist and feed onto the bobbin. If you can do this, then that hand already knows how to make a core! Now make sure your drafting hand can work the fiber to the side and not toward your body! (This part takes serious brain reprogramming.)

Spin!

Begin spinning a single in the normal way. When you are ready to core spin, break the roving off, leaving yourself about 4" (10.2 cm) of loose fiber. Fan this fiber out so it is not in a thick clump. Grab the inside line of fibers with one hand and use your drafting hand to pull the bulk of the fibers away from them at a 90-degree angle. Hint: Do not split the fiber into two separate pieces. Try and keep them webbed together in the shape of a fan.

Begin treadling, and then guide the twist through the inside fibers while pulling the remaining fiber away from the forming core. (This pulling away action is actually drafting the fibers.) Once you have pulled the fibers away from the core enough to draft them out,

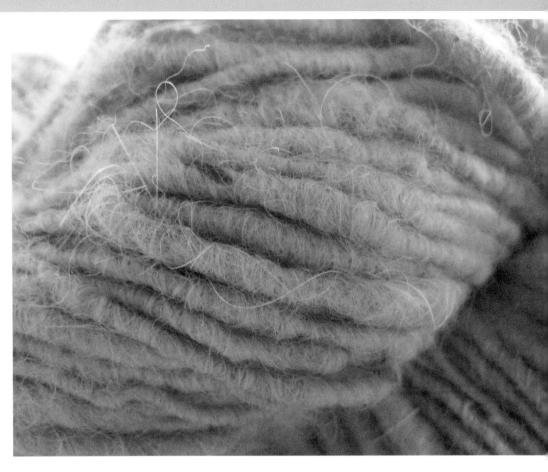
You should end up with the same horizontal grain as traditional core-spinning.

allow them to wind back onto the core. Feel the natural pull of the twisting core and let it wrap the loose fibers around the core fibers. Move down to the next bit of fiber and repeat.

As you spin, periodically tease core fibers out of the bunch with your non-drafting hand. I call this "scratching the kitty's chin." Don't laugh! That is exactly the movement you need to scratch a few fibers out at a time and into your palm to form the core. When you've spun that fiber, pull another small handful off your batt, and continue. Look for the telltale horizontal grain to see if you are doing it correctly.

Hint
DO NOT hold a lot of fiber in your hand at one time. This method only works by using very small bits of fiber at a time.

Core Spinning: Core Spots

Technically, anytime you have one fiber wrapping around another at a 90-degree angle, it's core spinning. There's no rule that says you have to core spin the entire length of your yarn. Try alternating between regular spinning and core spinning to get weight variations and color changes. Take this idea to the extreme and just core spin in one concentrated spot for a dramatic effect.

Materials
Contrasting fibers: one for the base yarn and different ones for the core-spun bubbles

Fiber Prep
Choose a slick, easy spinning fiber for the base such as silk. Select some loftier fibers for the bubbles—something light and airy with long enough fibers to be able to attach to the core, yet sit on top of the yarn in a voluminous way. I recommend carding in some mohair; it is perfect for this effect and it will help to trap the shorter staple fibers in the mix.

Spin!
Using the fiber you chose for the base yarn, spin a single in a traditional manner. When you are ready to add a bubble, break off the base-yarn roving leaving a couple of inches (centimeters) unspun at the bottom. Now grab a little pinch of the lofty carded fibers and lay one end of them into the unspun fibers of your yarn. Look for the directionality of the carded fibers and place them perpendicular to the base yarn. Begin treadling and guide the twist into one end of the bubble fibers. Use your other

hand to push the fibers onto the core. Once the bubble fibers have wrapped around two or three times in one spot, bring the tail end of the fibers down into the core fibers. Reconnect your base-yarn fiber and continue spinning as usual. Repeat for each bubble.

Note: See Coreless (page 70), for more in-depth instruction on how to control fiber in this manner.

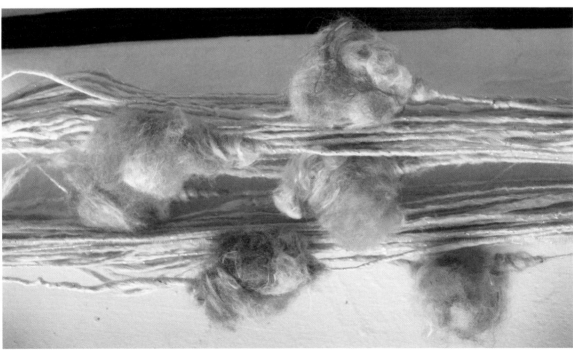

Core Spinning: Wrapped Yarn

This yarn is basically the opposite of core spinning. Instead of wrapping the fiber around a core thread, the thread gets wrapped around the fiber. The thread is now a decorative element instead of a structural one. Choose a thread that looks good with your fiber or has an interesting shape, pattern, or color. Any fiber will work for this technique.

Materials

4 oz [113 g] fiber or roving for base yarn

300 yds [275 m] novelty thread or lace-weight yarn

Spin!

Attach your roving and the thread to the leader and begin spinning a normal single. Spin a few inches (centimeters) with the thread spun into the fiber so that it is anchored. Now, take your hands off the thread and only spin the roving. As you spin, allow the thread to wind onto the yarn unencumbered between you and the orifice. Pretend that the thread is not even there. It will wrap around and around the yarn near the orifice. Sometimes it will backtrack on itself; sometimes it will jump ahead.

For the most part, you can just let it do its thing. Occasionally it may get stuck in one spot and need to be guided forward or backward. The *most important thing* is to make sure that thread is not under too much tension. Make sure it's on a cone or a spool that allows the thread to wind off easily without getting hooked up. If you have a ball of yarn or thread, put it in a bucket just under the orifice. The thread should have just the slightest bit of tension, as too much will just create knots. Repeat this process continually until the bobbin is full.

Note: You can also wrap strategic spots in the yarn instead of the entire length. Use this technique to create small areas of texture within the yarn.

Excerpted from Intertwined

Wrapped yarn

Orifice

Allow the thread to wrap on by itself. Do not touch it unless it gets stuck.

Spin normally.

Silk and camel thick-and-thin single wrapped in a delicate linen thread

Core Spinning: Sari Silk

There's no need to limit yourself to commercial yarns as core material. Try spinning a core with recycled sari silk. Sari silk consists of very long, strong threads that readily twist together. In theory, they are essentially many individual core threads twisted together! The bright colors of sari silk will show through when you use light colored or white mohair as your spinning fiber.

Materials
Recycled sari silk
White mohair, carded until light
  and fluffy

Spin!
Attach some sari-silk fibers to your leader thread and begin spinning a simple single. To draft sari silk you have to use a bit of muscle to yank on the threads until they thin out. Don't be shy about it! Once you get comfortable spinning straight sari silk, grab a small handful of the mohair. Pinch a few fibers of the mohair against the spinning sari-silk until it attaches. Then begin drafting the mohair away from the silk core at a 90-degree angle. Once the mohair is drafted out thin, allow it to wrap back onto the silk core very loosely. The difference in this technique is that the layer of mohair needs to be wrapped around very lightly so the colors of the sari silk show through.

Set the Twist

Soak the yarn in very hot water for twenty minutes, spin excess water out in a top-loading washing machine, and hang to dry with tension.

Core Spinning: Aura

This dramatic yarn, first shown in *Intertwined* (Quarry Books, 2008), is technically a core-spun yarn, only instead of the core being thin and the sheath (fiber spun around the core) comprising the bulk of the yarn, it's the opposite! For this yarn the core is spun big and fat and the sheath spun onto it is as thin as a web. For added interest a dark thread is used to wrap around during the process of spinning. Aura is a great example of how interesting a yarn can be when you take the techniques you know and then reverse them.

Miscellaneous hand-dyed, uncarded fiber

Materials
10+ oz (282.5 g) uncarded fiber, roving scraps, and semifelted wool in a variety of colors

2 oz (56.5 g) white mohair clouds

300 yds (274.5 m) novelty thread or lace-weight yarn

Fiber Prep
Place your collection of miscellaneous, uncarded fibers into a box or bag. Reach into the fiber and tease the locks and bits up somewhat—not too much because you don't want to lose the chunky texture of this project, but since you will be spinning these bits directly together you'll need some amount of teased/drafted fibers to connect it all.

Spin!
Using any old roving, spin a basic single for a few inches (centimeters) to give yourself a lead to tie off your skein later. This single should be long enough for tying off the skein. Now take the wrapping thread and tuck it into the fiber. Spin 3" to 4" (7.6 to 10.2 cm) to secure it. Grab a miscellaneous assortment of the uncarded fibers, roving bits, and semifelted wool and place them in your lap. Take a quiet moment to ready yourself for the challenge, breathe deep, open your eyes, and begin.

Randomly grabbing chunks from the fiber in your lap, begin spinning them together. Do not draft these fibers—simply spin them together in

their current state. While you do this allow the novelty thread to wind on between your hand and the orifice (See Wrapped Yarn page 74). Now for the tricky part: As you are spinning the uncarded fibers, grab small, thinly drafted clouds of mohair and allow it to loosely wrap onto the forming yarn (See Mohairy, page 68).

Everything should be happening simultaneously. Spin the uncarded fiber while fluffing the mohair around the forming yarn. In the meantime, the novelty thread is wrapping itself around the whole kit and caboodle near the orifice. Pay attention to the novelty thread to make sure it does not get stuck for too long in one spot. If it does get stuck, simply pull the thread forward with your hand until it begins to wind on evenly again. (The novelty thread will not wrap perfectly even, and the irregularity makes it unique—just don't allow it to get too concentrated in one spot.)

Continue the process until the bobbin is full. Wind the yarn off onto a niddy noddy. Tie in four or five places to prevent tangles, remove from the noddy, and soak in *very hot* water for fifteen to twenty minutes. Set yarn on yarn stretcher to dry.

Excerpted from Intertwined

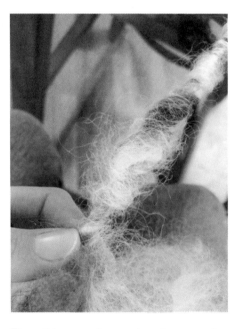

Three things are happening at once: spinning the uncarded fiber, surrounding it with mohair, and the novelty thread wrapping around the yarn close to the orifice.

Navaho-Ply: Basic

Navaho plying is a method of plying yarn that makes a three-ply yarn out of a solitary single. Prior to the Navaho and Pueblo people's use of it, it was known as chain plying in other parts of the world. Just as the name suggests, it is done by forming a basic chain from a single-ply yarn and twisting the chain in the opposite direction from the single was spun in. The main advantage to using the Navaho ply is that it preserves the colorway of the single as opposed to the barber-pole effect that happens when plying two different singles. Traditionally it was also thought that the Navaho ply was helpful in allowing you to even out your yarn by strategically matching thicker spots up with thin ones. (Now who would want to do that?)

Materials

Spinning fiber of your choice

Note: Don't begin with extremely short-fibered material such as cotton or down. Try wool, mohair, or silk until you get the hang of it.

Fiber Prep

Card a batt with the fibers of your choice or select some roving for your single.

Spin!

Spin a single as thin and evenly as possible. Spin it with a bit of extra twist, as the plying stage will take some of the twist out.

Ply!

Adjust your ratios to low twist and strong take-up (high tension). Remove the bobbin with your single and put it on a lazy kate or in a bowl at your feet. Place an empty bobbin on your wheel and tie a loop in the end of the leader on the bobbin. Also tie a loop into the end of the single that you just spun, then thread the loop of the single through the loop on the leader.

With one hand, open the loop of your single, reach through, grab the trailing single and pull a new loop through the original one. Pull the loop through approximately 12" (30.5 cm) or more if you can.

Navaho Ply

1.

2.

3.

Leader

Single

Pull loops through each other.

Spin the wheel in the opposite direction than the single was spun. The twist will begin to run up into the loop you have pulled through—be sure and bring an equal length of the trailing single along with the twisting loops so they all twist together, making a three-ply.

As the twist comes near the end of the loop that your hand is in, use that hand to reach through, grab the trailing single, and pull a new loop through. Repeat this chaining and twisting process until you have plied your whole single.

Note: Make sure your wheel is set for a strong enough take-up (increase tension). The yarn should be winding onto the bobbin as you spin. I find it helpful in the learning stage to stop treadling when you're pulling a new loop through. This will prevent over-twisting until you get the hang of it. Also, if your wheel is set up with scotch tension you may find it doesn't want

to wind on the bobbin when you pull loops. You may need to twist through a section, allow it to feed on, stop, pull a new loop, twist through, and then feed on, etc. It's not smooth but it gets the job done!

To end the yarn pull the last inch (2.5 cm) of the single completely through the last loop, loop it around, and tie it to itself in a knot. Also tie off the beginning of the yarn after it is wound off the bobbin to prevent the

yarn from coming undone (the same as a crochet chain can unravel).

Set the Twist

Soak the yarn in very hot water for twenty minutes, then place in a top-loading washing machine, spin to remove excess water, and then hang to dry. If the yarn is over-twisted, place a weight in the skein for tension or stretch between chairs to dry.

Navaho Ply: Thick and Thin

An extremely thick-and-thin single will expose the structure of the Navaho ply. Because the looped sections of your single are backtracked on themselves, the thick sections lose their gradual transition from thick to thin. Instead, the doubled up sections create an abrupt change from very thick to very thin. The same happens with the color transitions in your single. A normal single will have gradual color transitions, but the Navaho ply results in distinct color blocks. Experiment with this effect by spinning several different colors into the single, or choose smooth, thin-spinning materials such as silk, and periodically add bulkier sections such as semifelted roving or fluffy mohair. Don't be shy! I've found everything looks awesome when it's Navaho plied, and you'll be surprised how it transforms the usual into unusually interesting yarn!

Fiber Prep
The goal is to make a thick-and-thin single, so select a couple of contrasting materials that will spin up differently, or choose a batt or roving that tend to have slubs.

Spin!
Spin a single, drafting some sections very thin, and don't draft other sections, leaving a bulky spot. If you're including semi-felted wool, add it in manageable pieces, and make sure there is a good connection between materials. It is a good idea to over-twist this single since bulky sections will be less sound! Don't worry about balance, the Navaho ply will take a lot of this twist out.

Ply!

Remove the bobbin with the thick-and-thin single and place it in a bowl or on a lazy kate at your feet. Put on a new bobbin, make a loop in the leader, and follow the instructions for Navajo Multi-Ply: Basic (page 80).

Note: Be aware that in Navaho plying the thick sections are up to three times as thick as in regular plying! Depending on your wheel and orifice size, it may not readily feed onto the bobbin. Set your tension high so that the take-up is strong. You will likely need to hand-wind the bobbin at times. If you have this problem, eliminate some of the work by pulling the largest loops feasible and spinning back into your lap as far as possible before hand winding. Bulky spinners with large orifices come in handy for this technique.

Set the Twist

Soak in very hot water for twenty minutes, place in a top-loading washing machine, and spin to remove excess water; hang to dry. If the yarn is over-twisted, place a weight in the skein for tension or stretch between chairs to dry.

> **Tip**
>
> For an even more dramatic Navaho ply, see "Navaho Multi-Ply Dope Rope" on page 88.

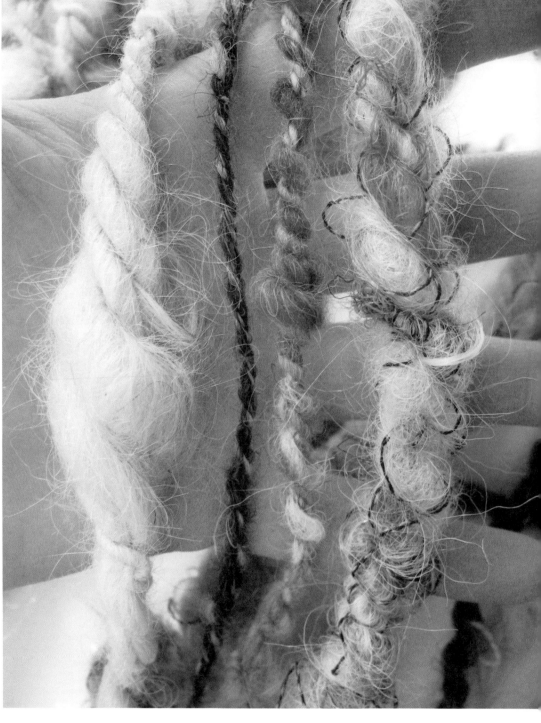

Spin different fibers and styles in your single and see how they transform!
Left to right: thick and thin alpaca; thin-spun natural wool; crazy carded batt; aura

Spinning Raw Fiber

Go ahead and call me weird, but I love working with raw wool. This may be an acquired taste—the equivalent of Limburger in the cheese world. Many spinners eventually develop an appreciation for spinning grease fleece and raw fleece. For me it strikes an even deeper chord than just getting used to it. Every time I open a bag holding a raw fleece, the moment the smell hits my nostrils I remember when I first learned how to spin. The first day of the class began with my teacher tossing a huge raw Romney fleece out on the floor at our feet. My introduction to spinning started, appropriately, at the beginning. It all starts with the sheep (or goat, or camel, or plant). Spinning raw fiber is as close to the source as you can get. It is a connection to the animal through the senses; it's the life and environment from which it came.

Raw wool also behaves in a different way from washed wool. The lanolin binds it together with a denseness that is hard to explain. The yarn has a very distinct hand. If you scrunch the yarn up, it stays that way for a second, and then slowly returns to rest. This action, its hand, the smell, the burrs, and dirt, are about as honest an experience with fiber as you can get.

Materials
Any raw fiber

Fiber Prep
If you are working with animal fiber be sure to skirt it, removing all sections with dung or excessive dirt and grime. Do not put greasy fiber through your carder unless it's a tough old machine and you're not worried about bent and greasy tines! Try spinning from the locks instead.

Spin!
You're on your own here. For me the fleece dictates how it wants to be spun. I recommend beginning with a handful, draft it when it gives, and let it be lumpy or have tails when it doesn't.

Ply?
Of course you can! Ply it on itself or try thread plying with a much thinner (but strong) material. This will accentuate the slow moving memory I talked about earlier. You can ply a little wiggle in there and the yarn stays that way!

I like to use raw fleece in my art shows, it makes the gallery smell like a barn (much to the gallery owner's chagrin) but it adds a fourth dimension to the work that wouldn't otherwise be there.

Spinning Large: Semifelted Dope Rope

If you have a wheel that can handle it, big rope-like yarns can be fun to make and add astounding pop to simple projects. They don't even need to be knit or crocheted, use them alone as a strap to a bag, curtain ties, or a dramatic trim to a coat or boots. Or, just hang them on your wall as a fiber sculpture.

Keep your eyes open at yard sales or antique stores for those big, heavy, box-framed plying machines with large orifices and bobbins as big as your thigh. Or try your hand at a great wheel with a quill. Some modern wheels are designed for these bulky styles as well. The main thing to look for is a big orifice and substantial take-up.

Spinning Large: Semifelted Roving

How many times have you pulled an old ball of roving or fiber out of your stash only to find that it has become partially felted? Well, don't throw it away! Use it to make a sturdy textured rope. For this technique you will spin two singles with this felted fiber, and then ply them together.

Materials

1 lb (0.5 kg) semifelted fiber. (If working with 8 oz (226 g) bobbins, allow for enough fiber to fill two bobbins; each one will be a ply.) Use only partially felted fiber. You will need to pull out and draft some fibers so you can connect one piece to the next.

Spin!

Using regular unfelted fiber, begin spinning a normal single to tie your skein off with later. Choose a piece of semifelted fiber, fluff up the ends and spin into the fiber you were spinning. Once it's connected, spin through the semi-felted piece. The semifelted fiber is already fused together to some degree, so you don't need a lot of twist to keep it together, and over-twisting will make it denser. Increase your tension for a good, strong take up. Focus on getting enough twist when connecting two pieces, but don't sweat it in-between. This is only one of the plies, so don't make it so bulky that it won't pass through the orifice in the plying stage.

Connect piece after piece until you have spun a full bobbin's worth; set aside. Repeat the process to fill a second bobbin.

Ply!

If you have a big bulky plying machine, now would be the time to use it! If not, you may have to ply half of the bobbin, then skein off, and finish the second half on a clean bobbin. Begin plying as usual with your wheel set to low twist and strong tension. If your wheel cannot accommodate the yarn, you may have to ply a few feet, stop, and then hand-wind onto the bobbin.

This yarn includes one ply made from a natural black and gray fleece that was partially felted during washing. The other ply was made from a selection of dyed semi-felted rovings.

Set the twist!

Soak your skein in very hot water for thirty minutes, transfer to a top-loading washing machine, and spin to remove excess water. Hang to dry with tension if the yarn is over-twisted.

Spinning Large: Navaho Multi-Ply Dope Rope

Navaho plying is bulky times three!

If you want to get bulky there's no quicker way than to Navaho ply. Navaho plying makes a three-ply out of a single. For this "dope rope" we are going to combine multiple singles and then Navaho ply them together. Navaho plying requires a lot of yardage, so spin extra to begin with if you are worried about not having enough.

Materials

Fiber of your choice! The sky is the limit. Spin singles in any fiber you want. They can be similar weights or dramatically different—that design choice is up to you.

Note: It is possible to use yarn other than singles; try throwing in an already spun two-ply. It is good to have one or two newly spun singles because the fresh twist plies easiest.

Spin!

Spin three separate singles. Make one or two of them very bulky. (The bulky is to make the dope rope. You can scale this down and make six- and nine-ply yarns with thinner singles, it's just as fun!) Place the singles near each other on a lazy kate. (If you don't have enough bobbins, wind the singles into balls, and stage them in bowls at your feet.) If you have a bulky head or a big plying wheel, do the Navaho plying on that.

Tie a loop in your leader string. Tie the ends of all three singles together in one loop. Pull the single's loop through the leader loop and follow the directions on page 80 to Navaho ply them.

clockwise from lower left: "Treasure Box" yarn two-ply wool yarn by Sandy Ryan (Homestead Wool and Gift Farm), and a super thick-and-thin salmon pink Icelandic wool single (mostly guard hair).

Note: This yarn may be very bulky in places, if the take-up on your wheel does not pull the yarn through the orifice, stop and hand-wind the bobbin.

Set the twist!

It's not imperative to set the twist in this plied yarn. I usually do though, especially if the yarn is over-twisted. Do set the twist if you plan on cutting it and letting it hang free (as in a fringe). Soak your skein in very hot water for thirty minutes, transfer to a top-loading washing machine, and spin to remove excess water. Hang to dry with tension if the yarn is over twisted.

Lexi's Tips

Beginning and ending yarns: It is helpful, especially with the really thick, dramatic yarns, to spin normally for a foot (30 cm) or so when you begin, and also when you end, your yarn. This section will be easier to tie off with when bundling your skein. This is also helpful because that first join, where the leader meets the new yarn, sometimes has trouble feeding into the orifice. It's always a good idea to get a bit started on the bobbin, making sure everything is working properly, before you launch into a more-complicated technique.

Best-ever core material: Commercial mohair yarn. I can't repeat this enough. It's thin, but it's strong, and all those grabby mohairs do a great job of attaching your fiber to the core.

Setting the twist without soaking the yarn: If you have objects in the yarn that you don't want to soak (feathers, for example) you can go a long way toward relaxing the yarn and setting the twist by steaming the yarn. Simply fill a tea kettle with water and bring to a boil. When steam is piping out of the spout gently pass the skein back and forth through the steam, holding it about 5 inches (13 cm) away from the spout. Hold the skein at each end, and let it gently loop into the steam. Rotate it around until all parts of the skein have been steamed. You should be able to see the yarn twisting around and settling in! Note: Be aware that some synthetics can melt and other fibers will scorch. Always start warily and move closer when you see that nothing is responding poorly.

Everything gets caught on my hooks! Yes, if only I had a dime for every time I heard that yelled in the middle of an otherwise pleasant workshop. Not to worry. A very simple fix is to remove the hooks from one side of your flyer, march them down to the hardware store and demand that the clerk replace them with the same diameter L-hooks. These are 90-degree angled hooks shaped like an *L*. They will hold the yarn in place but since they are not enclosed, bigger yarn will pass through them. Take them home and put them in every other hole. The fewer hooks you have, the less opportunity for "hook-ups."

I love luxury fiber, but there's no memory! To make sure you'll have a project that keeps its shape, adding some wool into the mix will help. I recommend adding 20 percent wool. You can still retain the look and feel of many nonmemory fibers such as alpaca, camel, and silk by choosing a wool that is very close in color to what you are working with.

Adding things in: Whenever you want to add something into the fiber you are currently spinning, be sure and draft a thin spot first! Thin spots attract twist; thick spots don't. Never try and add something to a fat spot. It'll just fall out. This goes for adding anything: new fiber, beads and bobbles, fabric–everything!

Slow down and stop! Our bodies are trained to keep treadling no matter what. Normally, when spinning traditional yarn, everything should be smooth with no surprises so treadling on and on is just what you do. But you'll have to untrain your body to do some of these techniques. There's a lot of stop and start involved. When you want to add something in, stop. Add it in, and then continue. Struggling to learn a technique? Slow down. Treadle slowly while you figure out hand positions, etc. This will help you to relax and prevent extreme over-twisting.

Auto-wrap thread gets tangled in the orifice! If you have a wheel with a delta-style flyer or other wire-based protruding hook, you may find that your thread becomes a tangled mess when you try and do the thread-wrapping technique. The solution is simple: gravity! Pay attention to the angle at which your yarn is going into the orifice. If it is slanting down toward the orifice, then the thread will naturally travel down the yarn to the orifice and get tangled. Try lowering your hands so that the yarn is going in perfectly level. If this doesn't work, lower them a little more and you'll see that the thread begins to travel back toward you and away from the flyer.

Which direction do I spin in a multi-step yarn? Remember that in multiple-step projects, each consecutive step should be in the opposite direction than the prior step. So sometimes you'll be going clockwise, even though you're plying. If you're not sure, do a little test in the beginning where you spin a short section, and see if it looks right. Then stop and go in the opposite direction. It will unwind and then rewind. See if the second version is balanced and looks better.

Core Spun + Quick-Coiled

92

Chapter 4

Permutations Gallery: Putting It All Together

In prior chapters and books (*Intertwined* Quarry Books, 2008 and *Handspun Revolution* Pluckyfluff, 2004) we've covered a lot of individual techniques. These may be fun to spin on their own, but combine them and you have exponential exhilaration! All of the ideas that have been presented are to help open the doors of possibility. To get spinners to feel comfortable with taking risks and to dispel the notion that failure is something to be feared. You can't fail when you're experimenting. The following gallery shows just a few of the astounding things that happen when you combine two or more techniques together. Try some combinations of your own devising. Use the basic techniques from these books or, better yet, come up with some of your own! What have you got to lose?

Seeding (Core Spun
+ Quick-Coiled +
Navaho Plied)
Lavendar Blingpaca fiber, by
Stephanie Gorin of Loop Fiber
Yarn by Pluckyfluff

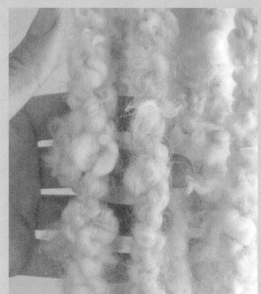

Tail Spun + Navaho Plied

Core Spun Fluffy + Navaho Plied

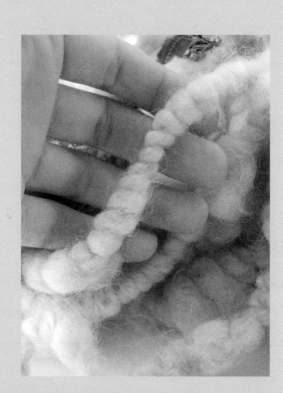

Tail Spun + Navaho Plied

Core Spun Fluffy + Quick-Coiled
Yarns by Ashley Martineau of Neauveau Fiber Arts

Aura
Mohair core spun over semi-felted fleece + wrapping

Aura + Navaho Plied

Mohairy + Wrap
Yarn by Kris Superiz,
Australia

Thick-and-Thin + Quick-Coil + Wrap

Chapter 5

Projects: Keeping It Simple

The following projects are designed for the express purpose of showing off the inherent qualities of the unique yarns that you spin. In general, you will find the patterns to be shockingly simple. But if you've taken the time and effort to instill extra character into the yarn, why undo all that work by hiding much of the yarn within a tricky or tight stitch? Simple knits, dropped stitches, and open weaves will give your yardage the most face-time. Each project was inspired by the yarn—the yarn dictated the item it wanted to be and the manner in which it should be made. Use these patterns as a starting point, but allow your own yarn to be what it wants to be. If it seems as if the yarn needs a little tighter stitch or some variation to really show off the elements that you've created, well then, do right by your yarn and adapt! Remember, in creative spinning you are imbuing the yarn itself with life and if you decide to transform it into a new object, let the method you choose serve to further express that beauty.

Easy Felted Fleece Rug

Do you love the look of sheepskin rugs? Here is a simple method for turning a beautiful shorn fleece into a rug or throw without having to kill the animal to do it. The final material you get from this looks great as is, but consider using it to cover throw pillows, line baskets, or trim a coat collar—you name it!

Materials

One whole unwashed wool fleece
Large stockpot of boiling water
Liquid dish soap
Heavy rubber cleaning gloves
Darning or sharp hand needle
Strong darning yarn

Size

Depends on the size of the fleece

Fiber

Any fleece from a breed that readily felts will work for this project. Make sure it is unwashed and as intact as possible. If the wool is washed it has likely lost its fleece shape. Avoid using a fleece that has already been pulled apart; it will be difficult to piece back together. Furthermore, it's the fibers that are naturally connected that make felting easy.

Felt Prep

Set the water to boil. Meanwhile, lay the raw fleece outside on a clean cement surface and skirt it, removing all unsightly wool, dung, or overly dirty parts. Turn the fleece over so the shorn side is facing up and the tips of the locks are against the cement. Drizzle dish soap lightly over the entire surface of the fleece. Don't go overboard with the soap; you need just enough to produce a little lather.

Felt It!

Once the water has boiled, bring the pot to where the fleece is. Using a cup, bowl, or ladle, scoop the hot water over a square foot (0.1 sq. m) area of the fleece, starting at an edge. Wearing the gloves, vigorously work the hot water and soap across the fleece surface. The wool should readily begin to felt under your touch. Once you've established the beginnings of felt with your hand, you can then use a bristle brush. Be very careful to concentrate the friction across the surface of the fleece rather than digging down into it. The idea is to felt the backside of the fleece while preserving the integrity of the nice locks on the other side. *Note: A fleece with longer locks tends to survive the felting process better.*

Work your way through the entire fleece, one square foot (0.1 sq. m) at a time. Don't worry if there are a few thin spots or holes. These will be fixed in the following steps. Once the whole fleece is felted, let it sit to dry.

Sew It!

Prepare to stitch together the weak spots of the dried fleece. Select a long darning needle with a large eye and sharp point. For thread, use a traditional darning material such as thin, strong, coarse two-ply wool. Thread the needle and even up the ends so you're sewing with a doubled thread.

With the felted side faceup, look for thin spots, gaps, or separations in the fleece. Stitch these back together using an overcast stitch, or any stitch you are comfortable with.

Once all the weak spots are stitched together, fill a large basin or tub with hot water, and gently submerge the fleece to begin the washing process. Wash the fleece as if you were going to spin it; gently soak and rinse it until the water runs clear. Put the rug into a top-loading washing machine and spin to get rid of excess water; lay out to dry.

Washing-Machine Boa

This is a shamefully simple way to make a gorgeous boa! Without fail, at every workshop I've presented, at least one student comes in distressed over having terrible results from washing a raw fleece for the first time. "It's ruined!" they say. And then, they pull from their bag a beautiful, dramatic, furry boa that would sell for $1,000 (£ 622) at Barney's. (I usually offer to take it off their hands.) After many years of interviewing these students about their so-called mistakes, I've learned how not to wash a fleece—and how to make a great boa!

Materials

Start with a beautiful raw fleece. If you use an unattractive fleece the result will be an unattractive boa. This project is all about the fleece, preserving the fleecy qualities and keeping it as close to its original state as possible. Staple length counts. I have found that short staples tend to felt into a skinny lumpy thing, so select a fleece that has medium to long locks. You can use mohair, wool, or alpaca. (If using alpaca, stick to long staple, and less a fine grade.)

Tip

It's almost impossible to tell tips from the base with alpaca, so don't worry about it. Also, for a daintier boa, put only one layer in the washing machine.

Fiber Prep

Lay the fleece out on the floor and skirt it of all unusable parts; short cuts, gummy wool, and any really muddy or dung-coated areas. From the remaining fleece, choose the parts with the most pristine and individual locks, and pull these sections out in strips wide enough to cover the bottom of the washing-machine tub. Keeping the locks attached to each other will make them felt together more smoothly.

Load the Washer!

Lay the fleece strips around the bottom of a top-loading washing machine keeping the fleece as intact as possible. When adding a section that is not attached, overlap a bit of the fleece already in the tub. Arrange two layers of fleece in the machine. For the best bonding results, place the first fleece layer with the tips of the locks face-down, and the second layer with the tips facing up. The base of the locks will felt together more readily than the tips. With the layers arranged base-to-base, it will give the boa a stronger core, and hopefully leave most of the beautiful tips sticking out.

Spin!

Set the machine for hot water and as small of load as is appropriate for the fleece. Too much water will allow the fleece to drift around too much. Usually small or medium load levels will suffice.

Add ¼ cup (60 ml) laundry detergent to the water, and then allow the fleece to soak in the hot water for ten minutes. (This will remove most of the dirt.) Agitate for two minutes, and then stop the machine.

Advance the dial to the spin cycle and spin out the excess water. One of the mistakes students make when trying to wash fleece, but that results in a great boa, is to have the machine start spinning before the water has fully drained. A whirlpool is created that gently twists the fleece into the form of a boa. Spin until all excess water is removed.

Fill the machine again with hot water, but this time don't soak the fleece. Agitate the fleece for two more minutes, stop the machine, set the dial to spin, and spin to remove the water.

Check the boa to see if it has bonded and the locks still look nice—not getting too felted. If it seems stuck together for the most part, take it out of the machine. If it does not seem bonded and is not felted at all, then repeat the hot water/agitate/spin cycle until the boa is to your liking.

Finishing the Boa

Lay the boa out on the floor in a line. If it is bonded in a circle, find a weak point and pull it apart. This is where the designing comes in. Look at the shape of the boa and decide where it needs more or less body. You will see weak areas where it may be barely connected. To make the boa stronger, tie some of the locks together with a square knot. Don't worry; no one is going to notice a little old knot in this big furry thing! Make sure the locks you are tying are securely attached to the core. If there are random lengths of boa shooting off in the wrong direction bring them in-line by knotting them to other parts. Work through the entire length of the boa, reinforcing weak spots with knots, and making a nice, somewhat uniform shape. When finished, give the boa a good shake to dislodge any loose pieces. Now throw it around your shoulders and hit the town—but be prepared for people to ask you when your show starts.

Artist Profile

Janice Rosema

Fiber Artist
San Diego, California

Janice considers all the characteristics of a given material and works to show them off. Cotted wool is transparant where it's thin. What many people would consider a weak point, or a flaw, Janice harnesses to bring vibrant life to the piece.

I met Janice a couple of years ago when she came by for a private class. I wondered why she was taking a class from me. I ended up learning so much more from her in the few hours we spent together. What struck me most about Janice was how comfortable she was in her artistry. She had settled long ago with the fact that she was a creator and an artist, and the path was never going to be easy, but she was ready to get on with it. And on with it she got. Janice has wandered through many nooks and crannies of the fiber-arts realm and there's probably nothing this woman couldn't, or hasn't made. I was particularly impressed by her crochet and knitted work; especially the pieces made from cotted wool (fleece that is slightly felted together). Janice is the kind of spinner I truly admire because her relationship with spinning has been multi-faceted. Today, she has the luxury of being able to spin whatever she wants, but there was a time when she spun to support her family. To have the ability to lean on your skills for survival, and then turn around and make those skills serve your creative whimsy, is the mark of mastery.

Q and A: Lexi and Janice

When and how did you come into fiber arts? Have you always done this innovative work, or did you start more traditionally?
Fiber arts have been part of my life since childhood. I remember designing and making doll clothes using my mother's old treadle sewing machine when I was about 5 years old. My grandmother was from another era and felt that young ladies needed to be taught the womanly arts of embroidery, knitting, crochet, and fine hand sewing. Learning these more traditional needle arts gave me the skills to follow my own creative visions.

As a spinner who has worked consistently through the waxing and waning of interest in spinning, what is your take on the present state of the art, versus the craft revival of the '70s or your grandmother's era?
When I was in my 20s I started spinning. Initially, my yarns were fairly traditional. As I discovered better quality wool, I graduated to a Pirtle bulk-production wheel. Then I discovered dyeing and things suddenly took off. My yarns were spun from the locks and had lots of texture and glorious colors. I was selling all over the United States, Canada, and France. At some point, I started making handspun knit sweaters for a Beverly Hills boutique. Today, there are so many options available for spinners in terms of materials, wheels, and dyes, that spinning is much more accessible to people.

Shawl made of cotted wool; crocheted by Janice Rosema

In the '70s, what I made was pretty unusual. Now, contemporary spinners run the gamut from very traditional to wildly artistic. I do think there is far more focus on the technical aspects of spinning now. Back then, I kind of flew by the seat of my pants. In my grandmother's day, none of the things I do now would have been acceptable. Then, finer work had more value to people.

Where have you found the most support for your work: Friends and family? Other spinners? The knitting community? Yourself?

In terms of support, I have kind of taken my own path and have been fortunate that people liked what I made. I have found the spinning community to be very nurturing with very few exceptions. The knitting and crochet communities are gradually learning how more contemporary yarns can be used in their medium—I find this very gratifying.

Have you worked in other mediums? Do you consider yourself a spinner, craftsperson, or artist first?

Over the years, fibers seem to predominate almost everything I have done. I design and create one-of-a-kind knitted and crocheted garments for boutiques and a select celebrity clientele. I spent quite a few years making hats (hand-blocked, knitted, crocheted, etc.) that sold in many high-end stores and boutiques throughout the United States and overseas. Also, I design patterns for using hand-spun yarns. Primarily, I would consider myself an artisan who spins.

What has been the biggest challenge in your creative endeavors?

When I began, my resources were very limited. Fortunately, I was persistent and loved what I was doing. Many things I created used found objects, materials nobody wanted. Necessity forced me to transform them into something of value that someone would consider buying. As I look back on this time, it really was a blessing because it made me be more creative using what I had available.

What is your greatest achievement?

My work has been featured in quite a few magazines, gallery shows, and exhibitions over the years. However, I think my greatest achievement is still to come.

If you could pick only ONE gem of advice for the rest of us, from a secret stitch to life's secrets, what would it be?

I believe it was Khalil Gibran who said, "Work is love made visible." This resonates with me, as the creative process requires a spiritual connection with what we do.

Whimsical and organic detailing

Knit shawl by Janice Rosema featuring tail-spun mohair yarn in earthy tones

Tell us a little about your process, especially with the cotted-wool pieces. Do you start with a plan or does it evolve as you go?

When I first saw a naturally felted fleece, it intrigued me for some reason. The shearers usually discard felted fleeces as they are considered unspinnable. Once the fleece was dyed, I laid it out on a table, and it sort of told me it was a shawl. I began using a variety of crochet stitches to reinforce some of the more open areas, and then began adding embellishments and leaves. Gradually, it evolved into the shawl that you see. I have more of these fleeces and each one is very different.

What inspires your designs? Are you driven by the material, emotions, or outside factors? Does your inspiration come from nature or culture?

In terms of inspiration, sometimes I see it in a dream and make a rudimentary sketch to work from. Often it is color that inspires me, or something I see in nature. Recently, I learned that hundreds of years ago Scottish and Irish men wore fleeces (not pelts) on their shoulders over their garments. Hmmm, it may have been ancestral voices calling me to create these shawls with a modern twist.

Plain-Skein Cowl

There will be times when the yarn you're spinning is beautiful just as it is. If you feel that knitting, crochet, or turning the yarn into a project would cause it to lose something, then leave it as it is! A skein of yarn is already the perfect size for an infinity scarf or cowl. Simply tie around the skein in at least three places and you're good to go. Tie the skein with sections of the yarn, or get fancy and tie it with ribbons, fabric, or other materials as an accent.

Tail-spun kid mohair locks in natural beige. Fiber from Fancy Fibers Farm

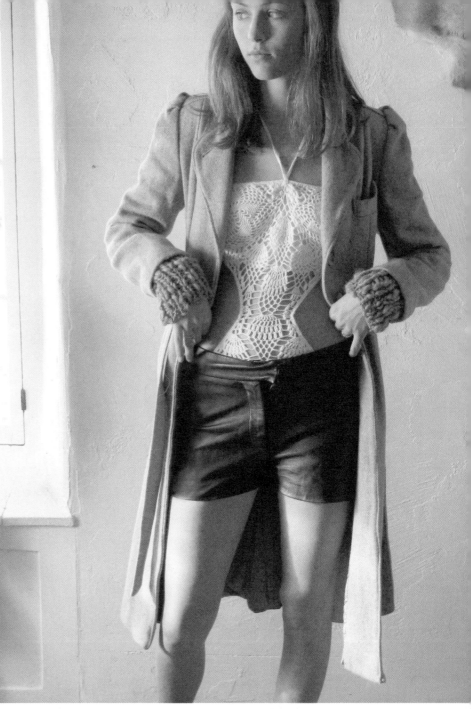

Vintage Coat Cuff

I don't know what they put in the water these days but it seems as though people just get bigger and bigger. Anyone with a weak spot for vintage garments knows the frustration of trying to squeeze a size-nine foot into a size-tiny heel. Granted, back in the day they had fewer vitamins and more corsets, but there is still hope for wearing those great vintage pieces in style. The following is a quick, simple, and satisfying solution for those vintage coats that fit great, are beautifully tailored, yet have sleeves just short enough to make them unwearable.

Knitting Skills Required

Cast on (CO)
Knit (k)
Purl (p)
Bind off (BO)

Size

Length 5" [12.5 cm]
Width 11" [28 cm]

Materials

Vintage coat
80 to 100 yds [73.2 to 90.5 m] hand-spun yarn
Size 10 (6 mm) set of 3 double-pointed needles

Darning needle
Strong yarn for sewing

Gauge

8 sts = 4" [10 cm] using size 10 [6 mm] needles in k1, p1 rib

Fiber Prep

Select a fiber with a coordinating color that will spin into a style of yarn that will complement the coat. If you want a really bulky thick-and-thin yarn, for example, don't reach for ultra-fine silk or downy fibers.

Spin!

Spin a yarn in the style you envision looking best with the garment. Remember, you will wear it so make sure it's something that will knit up to be flexible and not scratchy or irritating to the skin. (This is probably not the project for steel wool.)

Soak and set the twist of the finished yarn; hang to dry.

Cuffs (Make Two)

Using double-pointed needles, CO 22 sts. Divide sts onto three double-pointed needles; join sts in a circle taking care not to twist sts. Work around in k1, p1 rib for 5" [12.5 cm] or desired length. BO all sts.

Stitch

Pin one cuff inside a coat sleeve about 1" [2.5 cm] from the edge. (This will provide a nice overlap and hide your stitching.) Carefully turn the coat sleeve inside out.

Using a darning needle and a thin but strong yarn (or a thick sturdy thread), stitch the cuff pinned edge onto the coat. If the coat has a silk liner, try to stitch through the liner and into the coat material, but not all the way through. You don't want the stitches to show on the coat's right side. Stitch all the way around the cuff and tie off the yarn or thread.

Repeat with the second cuff.

A hand spun art
yarn design by
Michelle Snowdon,
wooldancer.etsy.com

Throwing Snowballs Neck Cozy

This neck cozy was inspired by my children's wish to create a gift for a friend during snow season and by my endless quest to create strikingly visual wearable accessories that best display the color and luxurious textural uniqueness of hand-spun yarn. This beautiful cozy adds a layer of warmth for adults and children alike!

This pattern requires basic skills which all knitters will be able to use, including newcomers using hand-spun yarn for the first time! It includes a lovely bind off that leaves a decorative ridge finish along the join. If you're not up to it, bind off stitches as usual, and seam the join.

The hand-spun yarn is spun to a snowball theme, however, any hand-spun yarn will do nicely. Throwing Snowballs uses a bulky two-ply hand-spun yarn with a gauge of approximately 6 wpi. You can spin the yarn and knit this up in about an hour!

—Michelle Snowden

Knitting Skills Required
Cast on (CO)
Knit (k)
Bind off (BO)

Size
Length: 20" [51 cm]
Width: 4" [10 cm]

Materials
2 oz [56 g] hand-carded batt consisting of hand dyed Australian merino, glitz and Angelina sparkle plied with a coordinating cotton spool thread
Size 10½ [7 mm] needles
Large stockpot of boiling water
Liquid dish soap
Heavy rubber cleaning gloves

Spin It!
To make the snowballs spin a few white Ingeo corn-fiber slubs into the singles yarn, and then spin snowballs using the beehive-coil technique (*Intertwined*, Quarry Books, 2008) during plying, or any dramatic, highly textured technique. You can knit this yarn right off the bobbin!

Knit It!
Using size 10½ [7 mm] needles, or size needles for a snug, but not stiff gauge for your hand-spun yarn, CO 9 sts. Work in garter stitch (knit every row) slipping the first st of each row for 20" [50 cm].
BO using three-needle BO, or your preferred method.

Three-Needle Bind-Off
For a lovely decorative bind-off, select a third needle one size larger than the 10½ [7 mm] needles, and work BO as follows.

Thread a 10½ [7 mm] needle through CO sts (you should now have 9 live sts on each of two needles). Bring the needles together, one in front of the other. Insert the larger third needle knitwise into the first st on the front needle and the first st on the back needle, knit these 2 sts together, *k next st from each needle together, pass the previous st over the last knit st; repeat from * across. Pull the yarn through the last stitch and tie off.

Cozy up your little snow bunny's neck and go throw some snowballs!

The One-Pound Three-Hour Scarf

Do you have somewhere to go tonight and you're sick to death of all your clothes? Here is a show-stopping scarf that you can make in three (yes, three!) hours, start to finish.

Knitting Skills Required
Cast on (CO)
Knit (k)
Purl (p)
Bind off (BO)

Size
Length: 84" [2.1 m]
Width: 8" [20.5 cm] slightly stretched

Materials
1 lb [453 g] ball of roving
One spool or cone of thread or thin
  yarn for striping (Or use a ball of thin
  decorative yarn left over from another
  project.)
Size 19 (15.5 mm) needles

Gauge
5 sts = 4" [10 cm] using size 19
[15.5 mm] needles in k1, p1 rib
(slightly stretched)

Fiber Prep
There is none! Who has time for that?
Use a roving that is already prepared,
combed, and in a ball ready to go.

Spin!
Attach the decorative thread to the
leader string before you start, and allow
it to spin along with the roving. Spin
a single from your roving. The thread
will make a nice candy stripe around
the yarn. The main goal is to spin a very
bulky yarn to ensure quick knitting
later. To do this, just barely draft. Every
few inches (centimeters), draft a thin
section but let lots of big chunky slubs
go through. Spin as quick and bulky as
possible. This should take about one-
half hour.

*Note: If the yarn was spun quick and soft
you shouldn't really need to set the twist.*

*But if you have the time, soak and set as
usual, and knit the following day.*

Scarf
Using size 19 [15.5 mm] needles,
CO 10 sts. Work in k1, p1 rib until
scarf measures 28" [71 cm] from CO.
Increase 1 st at each edge of next row to
compensate for the elongating that inev-
itably happens with heavy scarves—12
sts. Continue in established rib until
boa measures 56" [142 cm] from CO.
Decrease 1 st at each edge of next
row—10 sts. Continue in established
rib until scarf measures 84" (2.1 m)
from CO. BO all sts. Weave in ends.

*Note: The knitting should take a bit over
two hours to complete.*

Two-ply Shetland
wool yarn spun
in the lanolin by
Paul Verette

Cabin Hat

This is a great project for those of you who live in cold, damp climes. Made with yarn spun in the lanolin, this hat is extra warm and slightly water resistant! This example is made in a beautiful chocolate brown natural Shetland wool, but any natural wool would lend itself to this cozy cap.

Knitting Skills Required
Cast on (CO)
Knit (k)
Purl (p)
Knit 2 together (k2tog) decrease
Purl 2 together (p2tog) decrease
Bind off (BO)

Size
Circumference: 22" [56 cm]
Length: 13" [33 cm] unrolled; 8" [20.5 cm] with lower edge folded

Materials
About 120 yds [110 m] two-ply natural colored wool yarn spun in the lanolin
Size 9 [5.5 mm] set of 5 double-pointed needles
Tapestry needle

Gauge
15 sts = 4" [10 cm] in k4, p4 rib using size 9 [5.5 mm] needles

Hat
Using double-pointed needles, CO 80 sts. Divide sts onto four double-pointed needles; join in circle taking care not to twist sts. Work around in k4, p4 rib until piece measures 11" [28 cm].

Crown Shaping
Rnd 1: *K1, k2tog, k2, k2tog, k1, p8; rep from * 4 more times—70 sts.
Rnd 2: *K6, p1, p2tog, p2, p2tog, p1; rep from * 4 more times—60 sts.
Rnd 3: *K1, k2tog twice, k1, p6; rep from * 4 more times—50 sts.
Rnd 4: *K4, p1, p2tog twice, p1; rep from * 4 more times—40 sts.
Rnd 5: *K2tog twice, p4; rep from * 4 more times—30 sts.
Rnd 6: *K2, p2tog twice; rep from * 4 more times—20 sts.
Rnd 7: *K2tog, p2tog; rep from * 4 more times—10 sts.
Rnd 8: P2tog around—5 sts.
Cut yarn, leaving a 4" [10 cm] tail. Thread a tapestry needle with yarn tail and pass it through 5 rem sts. Gently pull yarn tail to draw sts together and close top of hat. Weave in yarn tails to WS and secure.

Earmuffs (Make 2)
Fold up the bottom edge of the hat 5" [12.5 cm] for brim. Place hat on head and mark placement at center of each ear. From the marked center st count 7 sts on either side—14 sts across. Pull a yarn loop through each of the 14 sts along the folded edge and place on needle.
Row 1 (RS): K1, p2, k to last 3 sts, p2, k1—14 sts.
Row 2 (WS): P1, k2, p to last 3 sts, k2, p1—14 sts.
Row 3: K1, p2, k2tog, k4, k2tog, p2, k1—12 sts.
Row 4: P1, k2, p6, p2, p1—12 sts.
Row 5: K1, p2, k2tog, k2, k2tog, p2, k1—10 sts.
Row 6: P1, k2, p4, k2, p1—10 sts.
Row 7: K1, p2, k2tog twice, p2, k1—8 sts.
Row 8: P1, k2, p2, k2, p1—8 sts.
Row 9: P1, p3tog twice, p1—4 sts.
BO.

Ties (Make 2)
Using three strands of yarn about 45" [114 cm] long, fold the strands in half, and working from the inside (WS) to the outside, pull the crook through a stitch at the bottom of one earmuff; pull the strands through the loop. Divide the strands into three groups, and braid; secure the bottom of the braid with an overhand knot. Ties should be about 22" [56 cm] long when braided.

Monkey Wrap

Here is a gorgeous open-knit shawl by Shannon Herrick of The Spun Monkey. Nothing shows off hand-spun yarn quite as well as dropped stitches and open patterns. Do you have a favorite yarn you have been saving for that perfect project? This might be it!

Knitting Skills Required

Cast on (CO)
Knit (k)
Knit in front and back of stitch (k1f&b)
Knit 2 together (k2tog)
Yarn over (yo)

Crochet Skills Required

Chain (ch)
Double crochet (dc)
Single crochet (sc)

Size

Work to desired size

Materials

Approximately 200 yds [183 m] bulky hand-spun yarn (or mixed wool core-spun yarn)
Size 35 [19 mm] needles
Size N-15 [10 mm] crochet hook
Giant stitch markers

Knit!

Using size 35 needles, CO 1 st.
Row 1: K1f&b of st—2 sts.

Row 2: K1f&b, pm (place marker), k1f&b—4 sts.
Row 3: K1f&b, k1, sm (slip marker), k1, k1f&b—6 sts.
Row 4: K1f&b, yo, k2tog, sm, k2tog, yo, k1f&b—8 sts.
Row 5 and every odd row: K1f&b, k to marker, sm, k to last st, k1f&b—2 sts increased each odd row.
Row 6 and every even row: K1f&b, k to 2 sts before marker, yo, k2tog, sm, k2tog, yo, k to last st, k1f&b—2 sts increased each even row.
Repeat Rows 5 and 6 until the wrap is desired size (the crochet edge will add about 1" [2.5 cm] to the top and 1½" to 2" [4 to 5 cm] on the sides) or until you have about one-third of your yarn left. End on an odd numbered row. BO with remaining yarn but DO NOT cut.

Crocheted Scallop Edging

Using size N-15 hook and beginning at last st of BO, work along the two sides, and then across the top of the wrap as follows: (Ch 2, dc, ch1, 2 dc) in first st, *ch 3, skip next st, (2 dc, ch 1, 2 dc) in next st; repeat from * along two sides. Then working across top of the wrap (BO row), ch 2, sc into each st across top skipping a st as necessary to maintain the correct width without puckering. Fasten off.

Weave in your ends and block your finished wrap!

First grade class from Cedar Springs Waldorf School, Placerville, California, with their finger-crochet project.

Finger-Crochet Table Runner

Attention Teachers!
This table runner is a great project for a family or first-grade class!

This project came about while working with a first grade class at Waldorf School. What began as an introduction to finger crocheting, ended up in this fantastic collaborative piece. Try this at home with your school-age children to familiarize them with yarn and expose them to the joy of working together on a common goal.

This project consists of two yarn types. The majority are simple, single spun yarns in solid colors. For accent there are variegated two-ply yarns made from a carding session with the children.

Spin!

Pick your solids! For the bulk of this project spin some very simple, balanced, and even single-ply yarns in colors that the children like. I suggest making this yarn the basis for the project because it will be easy for young children to handle, thus cutting down on frustration levels!

Mix it up!

For a textural accent and to introduce the children to the concepts of carding, color, fiber, and spinning, stage the following event. Lay out a large selection of fibers, making sure there are different colors and textures. Position a drum carder at the end of the table. Allow each child to walk along the table and select fibers they like. (If it is a large class, you only need one-half ounce or so per student.) Have each child bring their fiber to the carder and watch you arrange the fibers for carding. If they are 7 or younger it's probably best that they don't get near the drums, but let them do the cranking! Allow each child to make a little batt.

Spin It!

Taking turns, have each child bring you their batt for spinning. (Since most first graders don't spin yet, just take this opportunity to demonstrate.)

Allow the child to assist with tearing fiber from the batt. Stop and show them the interesting color combinations or textural parts that come up. This is a great opportunity to compliment them on their interesting choices! Really get them involved by emphasizing their contribution to the process.

Note: Spin each child's batt onto the same bobbin, creating one yarn made from the individual contributions. This will emphasize the notion of collaboration.

When all the fiber is spun, ask the children for thread-color suggestions to ply the yarn. Or Navaho ply the yarn on itself (see page 80 for instructions).

Collection of finger-crocheted chains ready to be sewn

Crochet It!

The crocheting takes place over a few weeks' time. Have the children finger-crochet lengths of basic single chain, eventually using up all the yarn. A finger-crochet chain is made the same way as with using a crochet hook, only the children pull the loops through with their fingers. There's no need to specify the length, and they can work on them during down times. The children can watch their collection of chains build up over time!

Sew It!

Once you have a substantial number of chains, prepare to sew them together (you can arrange them side by side to estimate how wide the runner will be). Since this project in inherently mul-

ticolor, try using a randomly colored selection of sewing threads to connect the chains.

Arrange the chains in order from short to long. Beginning with the two longest pieces, place them side by side on the bed of the sewing machine. Make sure the chain right side is facing up! Set your machine to a horizontal stitch. I set the width to 5.5 or 6.0 and the length to 1.0 (depending on the thickness of your chains you may need to adjust the setting).

Start stitching a few inches [centimeters] from the ends to establish a fringe, and stitch back and forth a couple times to make a knot. Sew the chains together, making sure the needle is catching the edge of each chain evenly. Stop a few inches (about 7 cm)

Having a hand in the process plants the seeds of appreciation for the art of handcrafts.

Be sure the machine stitch is catching both chains! Notice the contrast of the textured yarn from the children's batt-making session. That pink poof was from a student's highly-textured batt.

Coasters

If you have any extra short or random chains, make some coasters to match! Use the same stitch setting, but instead of stitching a straight line, coil the chain around in a spiral as you sew. Make the coaster a solid color, or add a different color for the outer ring.

from the opposite end, and then stitch back and forth to knot off. This sewn strip will be the center of your runner. Take the next shorter chain and add to one side. Add the next shorter chain to the other side, and so on.

Don't worry if the chains are different lengths. The runner will be longer in the middle and taper toward the ends. Leave plenty of unsewn fringe to add to the organic shape.

Once the chains are connected, go through the fringe and tie a tight knot where you want each chain to end, and then trim any ends that are too long or unsightly.

Use this runner for the classroom lunch table or your family table at home. Ask the children to see if they can spot their contributions in the final piece!

Namaste Farms Boa

If ever there was a pattern that let's the yarn speak, it's this one by Natalie Redding of Namaste Farms. With a bare minimum of knitted rows, this piece is all fringe! Using high quality mohair will ensure an intoxicatingly nice drape.

Knitting Skills Required

Cast on (CO)
Knit (k)
Bind off (BO)

Size

Length: 60" [1.5 m]
Width: 15" [38 cm]

Materials

Size 15 [10 mm] needles
80 yds [73.2 m] Namaste Farms Long
  Locks yarn or falling-locks yarn (see
  page 47 for spinning instructions)
1 skein worsted weight Caledon Hills in
  similar color to Long Locks yarn

Knit!

With worsted-weight yarn and knitting two strands as one, CO 98 sts, k 3 rows, BO. This is the base of the boa.

From the falling-locks yarn, cut fringe pieces as you work—not ahead of time. Cut the yarn into lengths as follows or as desired: 24", 20", 15", 12" [61, 50.8, 38.1, 30.5 cm]. Lay the knitted base lengthwise on a table with the wrong side facing up. Beginning at the ends, add fringe to the middle row of the base. Fold each yarn section in half, thread the fold through the middle row forming a loop, and then pull the ends through the loop. As you work toward the center of the boa make the pieces shorter and shorter.

Add more fringe to each end of the boa through the CO and BO rows as well, to make the ends fuller. The boa will be wider at the ends than in the neck area. The neck may be left bare, as shown, if desired.

Rocker Jacket

I was in a coffee house the other day and heard someone say, "Man, the denim jacket is really back, eh?" And I thought to myself, "Was it ever out?" You can never go wrong with what might be the most perfect clothing item ever created. And sheepskin or fur goes perfectly with old denim. The following is a good way to get the furry collar you want without having to sacrifice an animal to do it. Any long-locked wool will work for this project. Take a little extra time to find the color and length of fiber that looks best with the denim you're working with.

Materials
Denim jacket
Approximately 10 oz [28 g] long-staple
  wool, uncarded
Strong polyester-core thread
Sharp darning needle

Fiber Prep
The amount of yardage you'll need depends on the size of your jacket and how much of the lapel and collar you wish to cover. Do a rough estimate ahead of time to make sure you spin enough. Look at the length of your locks, and envision how thick the yarn will be. Then take a tape measure and run it around the edge of the collar the distance you want to cover; record that measurement. Envision how many rows of the shaggy yarn are likely needed to fill that space (positioned side by side in rows, parallel to where you measured, and not knitted or crocheted). Then

multiply your initial measurement by the number of rows. To be safe add a few extra yards.

To prepare your locks gently scour them according to the directions on page 17, and then let dry. Be extra careful to keep the locks intact as possible. The nice individual tips are what make the finished collar look good. Spin a shaggy tail-spun yarn; see "Extreme Tail Spin" on page 50.

Stitch!

Before you begin, lay strips of yarn on the lapel to get an idea of the optimal spacing between rows. Thread a needle with a doubled thread and knot the ends together; stitch into the denim beginning at the lowest point on the lapel that you wish to cover. Place a length of the shaggy yarn along the outermost edge of the lapel, loop the thread over the yarn, stitch back into the denim near the starting point, and cinch tight. Sew the next few stitches only into the denim to cover some distance; there is no need to loop every stitch over the yarn. Every five stitches or so, loop the thread over the yarn to tack it in place. If the core of your yarn is dense enough, run the needle through the yarn every few stitches to add strength.

After tacking the yarn around the outermost edge, loop it back, and continue tacking it next to the first row. You will continue in this back-and-forth manner until the collar is covered. You don't need to tack the rows overly close together if the locks are nice and long. They will fill in the space, and you shouldn't be able to see the denim through them.

Hint

If the collar consists of two denim layers (or has a lining), stitch only into the exposed layer. Avoid having the stitches visible on the backside if possible.

Pom-Paca Hat

Nothing shows off chunky handspun like simple patterns and shapes. Here is a very basic hat made intriguing by a thick-and-thin, slightly tail spun alpaca yarn.

Knitting Skills Required

Cast on (CO)
Knit (k)
Knit 2 together (k2tog) decrease
Stockinette stitch (St st): knit all rounds

Size

Circumference: 22" [56 cm]
Length: 8" [20.5 cm] without pom-pom

Materials

About 3 oz [85 g] natural colored alpaca
  fiber (The alpaca fiber should not be
  overly short and fine. You want some
  of the tips to remain intact and stick
  out for texture.)
Size 10 [6 mm] set of 5 double-pointed
  needles
Spool knitting elastic (optional)
Tapestry needle

Gauge

8 sts = 4" [10 cm] in St st using size 10
[6 mm] needles

Fiber Prep

Spin your alpaca fiber uncarded as a thick-and-thin single. Occasionally allow some of the tips of the fiber to stick out, but not too much, you want these as an accent but not to overwhelm the look of the yarn.

Soak, set, and allow yarn to dry.

Knit!

Using double-pointed needles and one strand of yarn and one strand of knitting elastic held tog, CO 42 sts. Divide sts onto four double-pointed needles; join sts in circle taking care not to twist sts. Work around in k1, p1 rib until piece measures 2" [5 cm]. Now using only one strand of yarn, change to St st, and k every rnd until piece measures 4" [10 cm] from CO edge.

Crown Shaping

Rnd 1: *K4, k2tog; rep from * 6 more times—35 sts.
  Rnd 2: K even.
  Rnd 3: *K3, k2tog; rep from * 6 more times—28 sts.
  Rnd 4. Knit even.
  Rnd 5: *K2, k2tog; rep from * 6 more times—21 sts.
  Rnd 6: Knit even.
  Rnd 7: *K1, k2tog; rep from * 6 more times—14 sts.

Rnd 8: Knit even.
Rnd 9: K2tog around —7 sts.
Rnd 10: (K2tog) 3 times, k1—4 sts.
Cut yarn, leaving a 4" [10 cm] tail. Thread tapestry needle with the yarn tail, and work yarn through 4 rem sts. Gently pull to draw sts together and close top of hat. Weave in yarn tails to WS and secure.

Pom-Pom

Cut approximately 20 strands of yarn 4" [10 cm] long. Tie the strands together in center to form a pom-pom. Pull the tie ends through the top of the hat and knot together on the inside.

Tip

Alpaca yarn does not have the memory to hold its shape like wool. For a tighter fit, work the ribbing with one strand of yarn and one strand of knitting elastic held together.

BFF! (Best Friends Fingerless Gloves)

Here is a fun project to do with your best friend. The idea is to start with the same materials but each of you will go your separate ways to make ONE glove in private. There will be no discussion of pattern or design, aside from the basic size parameters. Only the common threads will tie these gloves together. A good friendship is made strong by common interests and similarities, but kept interesting by differences of opinion or perspective. This pair of fingerless gloves embodies both of those things. By starting with the same materials and basic guidelines these gloves are unified, but the individual personalities shine through, making this a wearable representation of this important relationship.

This project might yield weird results if you and your best friend are psychically connected! When I conceived this idea I figured we would end up with two very different gloves. I knew I wanted to do a vertical stripe, and I thought my good friend Mindy would do horizontal stripes or blocks. I was predicting very different gloves. Then Mindy walked in with practically the same design as mine! I was speechless. To that she said, "Oh no, after you dropped off the yarn and described the project, I could picture these gloves in your mind. I was a little miffed too, because it was way out of my comfort zone. But it's what you wanted." Warning: beware of mind-reading friends.

Materials

Yards of any hand-spun yarn. Use one yarn or multiple ones. Consider using a yarn spun by each of you to make this project even more intertwined.
Several yards [meters] each of: single-ply 100% camel with sparkle (27 wpi), single-ply 100% musk-ox brown with sparkle (27 wpi), single-ply 100% silk natural yarn (34 wpi)
Sizes 6 [4 mm] and 8 [5 mm] straight needles
Size 6 [4 mm] and 8 [5 mm] double-pointed needles
Size H-8 [5 mm] crochet hook
Tapestry needle

Gauge

16 sts = 4" [10 cm] in St st using size 8 [5mm] needles and single strand of yarn for lacy effect
16 sts = 4" [10 cm] in St st using size 6 [4 mm] needles and double strand of silk with single strands of other two yarns for a less lacy effect

Lexi's glove is on top; Mindy's is underneath.

Knitting and Crochet Skills Required

Cast on (CO)
Double crochet (dc)
Single crochet (sc)
Stockinette stitch (St st), knit 1 row, purl 1 row
Bind off (BO)

Size

Length: 11" [28 cm]
Circumference: 8" [20.5 cm]

Guidelines

Agree on a general size for the gloves and whether they will be knit or crochet, but not much more. Perhaps stipulate if the fingers will be separated, or if there will be a thumb or just a thumbhole. Aside from that, the idea is to see what each of you will do with the same yarn without discussing it ahead of time. Decide who will make the right glove and who makes the left.

Make!

Now go your separate ways and make the glove in whatever fashion that suits your fancy. When you come back together you'll be surprised how good the gloves actually look together!

Lexi's Lacy Fingerless Glove

This glove is 11" (28 cm) long. You may need to figure the gauge for the yarn you're using to adapt this pattern.

With size 8 [5 mm] straight needles and single strand of brown musk ox, CO 44 sts.

Stripe Pattern

Working in St st: 2 rows in brown, 3 rows in natural, 2 rows in camel, and 3 rows in natural; changing to size 6 [4 mm] straight needles when working brown. Repeat these 10 rows until the piece is wide enough to wrap around your hand; BO. With the knitted piece wrapped around your hand, mark where the thumb opening should be. Crochet the seam together leaving the thumbhole open.

Hand and Thumb Edging

With crochet hook and natural, sc in next st, *(sc, 2 dc, sc) in next st for scallop; repeat from * around hand edge. Work the same edging around thumb opening.

Arm Edging

With size 6 [4 mm] double-pointed needles and brown, pick up and k approximately 36 sts around arm edge; divide sts evenly on needles. Join and work around in k1, p1 rib for 4 rnds; BO in rib.

Note

The natural silk yarn was substantially thinner than the other two, creating a nice lacy effect. The brown camel yarn was the thickest, so it was worked with a size 6 (4 mm) needle in order to bring more attention to that stripe.

from top to bottom: musk ox, silk (spun by Alanna Wilcox), and camel. Talk about luxury!

Mindy's Bold Stripe Fingerless Glove

Mindy worked two strands of silk together and used one strand each of the other two yarns, resulting in a more regular material. This glove is 11" (28 cm) long. You may need to refigure gauge for the yarn you're using to adapt this pattern.

With size 6 [4 mm] straight needles and single strand of brown musk ox, CO 44 sts.

Stripe Pattern
Work in St st: 4 rows in camel with single strand, 3 rows in natural with double strand, 3 rows in brown with single strand. Repeat these 10 rows until the piece is wide enough to wrap around your hand; BO. With the knitted piece wrapped around your hand, mark where the thumb opening should be. Crochet the seam together leaving the thumbhole open.

Thumb
With size 6 [4 mm] double-pointed needles and single strand of brown, pick up and k8 sts around thumb opening; divide sts evenly on needles. Join and work around in k1, p1 rib for 6 rnds; BO loosely in rib.

Hand Edging
With size 6 [4 mm] double-pointed needles and single strand of brown, pick up and k approximately 48 sts around hand opening; divide sts evenly on needles. Join and work around in k1, p1 rib for 8 rnds; BO loosely in rib.

Arm Edging
With size 8 [5 mm] double-pointed needles and single strand of brown, pick up and k approximately 48 sts around arm edge; divide sts evenly on needles. Join and work around in k1, p1 rib for 8 rnds; BO in rib.

Hint

The idea of making a single pair of gloves is poetic, but if you can't agree on who gets to wear them, you could each make two, leaving you both with a missmashed set. (Be sure to make a right- and a left-hand glove.)

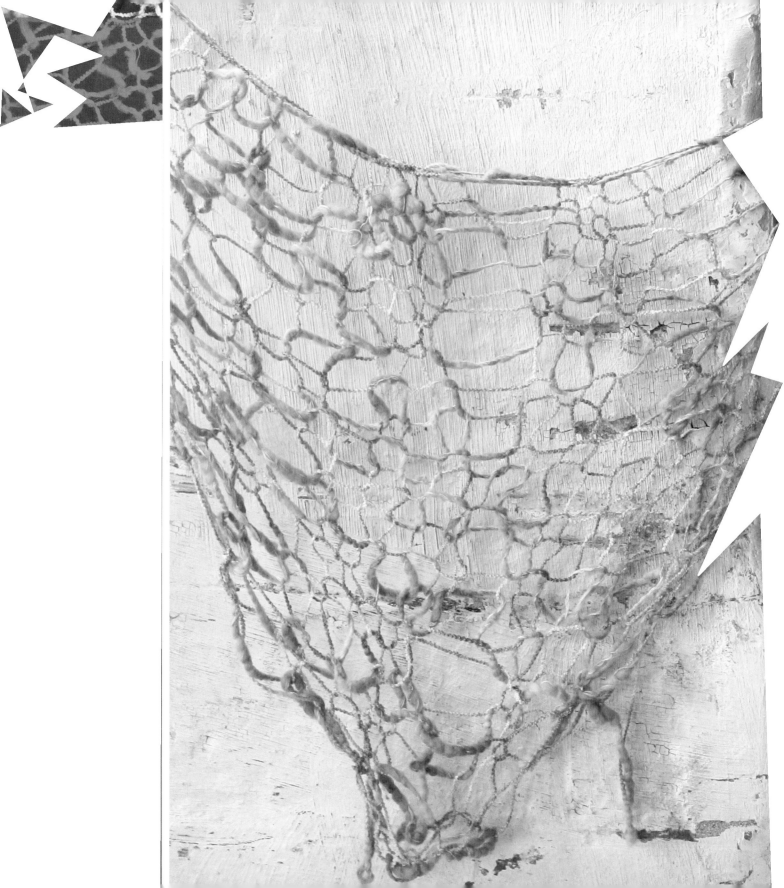

Webby Wrap

For a great organic-looking wrap try this simple pattern using an alternating slick-and-fat yarn. When you do an open-knit with a yarn that has fat, soft slubs alternated with thin, slick sections, you get this effect. The thin parts will slide together while the thick soft spots hold their shape. No tricky stitches required! This shawl was contributed by Val Pascall of Australia.

Knitting Skills Required
Cast on (CO)
Knit (k)
Bind off (BO)

Size
Width across top: approximately 52" [132 cm]
Length: approximately 23" [58.5 cm]

Materials
2 oz [1.8 g] carded wool
2 oz [1.8 g] silk (banana, Tencel, or any other very slick fiber)
Size 50 [25 mm] needles
Tapestry needle

Fiber Prep
Card the fibers together or spin them together without carding first, it's up to you. If you choose to card them first, run them through the drum carder in thick sections, and card the batt only once. The fibers must stay sufficiently separate in order to spin in an alternating soft/slick way.

Spin!
Spin a single using your combined batt, or alternate spinning the wool and the slick fiber. Try and spin the wool as a soft thick-and-thin. When you get to the slick fiber make an effort to spin it thin and even.

Knit!
With size 50 [25 mm] needles, or the largest you can find, CO 3 sts.
  Row 1: Knit.
  Row 2: Knit and CO 1 st at each end of row.
  Rep these 2 rows until wrap is desired width (approximately 31 sts), or until you run out of yarn; BO.
  With tapestry needle, weave in ends.

The Yarn

For this project the designer spun mid-gray fleece plied with darker gray commercial single, and then overdyed the yarn with Landscapes' quarry, moss, and rust.

Notes from the Artist:
Val Pascall

I was one of eleven children and had a very creative mother who taught us to do things with our hands. One saying she instilled in all was, "busy hands; a happy mind," which I still use. I enjoy teaching small children that their brain and their hands are the best tools they have.

Dear Lexi,

Regarding the birth of the "Webby Wrap," I was supporting some foster children at the Melbourne children's court. At the first session I started to knit with size 50 (25 mm) needles. Spectators of all ages, types, and nationalities looked on, asking about my project, so I showed them how to knit. This activity continued until the guards took my needles, saying they were a weapon! This made me very angry because I believe many of our young people are not inspired early in their lives, which is why so many young people go unchallenged in their artistic development.

After my needles were deemed a weapon, I returned the next week with two rulers and did the knitting on those. I wanted to challenge the stupidity of their act the week before.

Hope you can get something you can use.

Happy creating,

Val Pascall

Val Pascall with her ruler-knit shawl. Val is a fiber artist, spinner, and knitter who lives in Australia.

The "Unsinkable"

If there's one thing I enjoy doing as much as spinning, it's fly-fishing. I grew up fishing the trout waters of California's enchanting Sierra Nevada mountains. The small high-alpine creeks of the Sierras are hard to get to, icy-cold, and chock full of trout. It's not the kind of water you go to catch giant fish you can measure and brag about to your neighbor. The fish are small, and you have to hike miles to get to the creeks, which you can hop over in one leap. But the fish are feisty, beautiful, and go for one thing like a bat out of hell; a good dry fly.

There's one real important element that differentiates dry-fly fishing from other fly-fishing and I'll give you one guess as to what it is. That's right! The fly needs to be dry. And why do they need to be dry? So they float and look like a bug that just fell on the water. Normally, fishermen have to stop every few catches and goop up their fly with a greasy synthetic floatant to give it buoyancy. Flies are tied from natural animal fibers, traditionally using materials such as elk hair and feathers. These fibers don't resist water very well, thus the need for floatant. But one day, as I was sitting by the creek, accidentally dripping floatant all over my jeans, and in general struggling with the equipment and gear when it dawned on me: Why not spin a thread from greasy lanolin-rich wool and tie a fly from that? It looks super buggy, as we fisherman are fond of saying, since the lanolin makes it water resistent, you would never need to mess with the gross floatant again! It would be unsinkable! And there it was, plain as day. The "Unsinkable" was hatched.

Materials

You'll need to get some very greasy fleece in natural colors. Experiment with colors from cream to dark brown, as there are many natural insects in these colors. The main requirement is that the fleece should have plenty of natural lanolin in it. Don't worry about washing the dirt out of the fleece, the closer to a living thing the better when it comes to tricking fish. To give the fly even more life, card some iridescent and slightly shimmery fibers in with the wool. Don't go overboard with it, you want just enough that the thread has some iridescence similar to many bugs. This is why peacock feathers are very popular material for tying flies, they have that shimmery, dark green that real flies have. For the example pictured I chose some angelina and firestar synthetic fibers in green, dark blue, black, and a teeny bit of copper.

Spin!

Spin a single ply as thin as you can. Fly tiers use thread to make flies, they don't want to work with lumpy, bumpy, or bulky threads.
Soak and set the twist; let dry.

Unsinkables: three versions tied by Alex Stephens, Placerville, California

The Unsinkable in an Adams pattern. The hand-spun thread creates a segmented effect and it has some wispy strands that stick out. Instead of trimming these ends, a good fly fisherman knows that the more impressionistic a fly looks, the more real it seams to the fish. Brand new perfect flies don't catch half as many fish as the tattered old ones do.

Hint

When carding greasy wool use a heavy-duty old carder, the wool can really bend tines. Or use old hand carders, you don't need to prepare much fiber for a few flies.

Unsinkable Recipes
Alex Stephens

Ever since the Titanic, we've heard the term "unsinkable" being thrown around willy-nilly. Fortunately for anglers, the Unsinkable does not rely on exorbitant size to prevent it from sinking. By incorporating freshly spun greasy wool into traditional fly patterns, it eliminates the need for dry-fly floatant. The Unsinkable is destined to revolutionize the sport of fly-fishing. Bring on the iceberg!

Your's truly,
—Alex Stephens

Adams Unsinkable Pattern
Hook: mustad 94840
Thread: black 6/0
hackle: grizzly and brown, mixed
body: spun greasy wool
tail: grizzly hackle fibers
wings: grizzly hackle tips

Mayfly Unsinkable Pattern
Hook: mustad 94840
Thread: black 6/0
hackle: grizzly and brown, mixed
body: spun wool
tail: grizzly hackle fibers

Caddis Unsinkable Pattern
Hook: mustad 94840
Thread: black 6/0
body: brown hackle, spun wool
wings: elk hair

New Weave Belt

Here is a wrongly-woven belt that looks just right! For a fringe effect, set up the warp along the long edge and work the length as the weft. Use the featured belt as inspiration; these materials were collected from here and there. Look for your own interesting materials to combine for this fresh belt! Or to simplify your life, find a wide, soft second-hand belt to update with your weaving.

Skills Required
Intermediate weaving skills

Size
Length: 30" [76 cm] without fringe and belt rings
Width: 2" [5 cm]

Materials
Scrap wood larger than size of your belt
2½" [6.5 cm] finish nails
Yarn of your choice
For the belt pictured:
  Vintage woven fabric
  Soft sewable leather
  2 metal belt rings
  Pyramid studs

Make the Loom!
Draw a 25½" × 2" (65.8 × 5 cm) rectangle on your wood in the shape of the belt.

Hammer nails along the long edge, spacing them as close as possible to make a dense material. (This will depend on the yarn you are using. The pictured yarn is 12 wpi and nails are spaced every ⅛" [3 mm].)

Warp the loom by cutting short lengths of yarn you can easily knot around the nails. Each nail should have two strands knotted together around it. Warp the whole loom.

Weave!
Since this is a tight space to work in, make life easier by precutting some long strands for the weft. For the belt pictured, we cut a doubled strand of yarn the same length as the belt. Using a crochet hook and starting at one end of the loom, run the hook over and under the warp for a few inches (centimeters), hook into the crook of the long yarn, and pull it through. Then move ahead a few more inches [centimeters], weave the hook through, hook into the crook, and pull the yarn through some more. Be sure and gently pull up slack from the starting point as you go and work the yarn through the whole distance. Pull a few inches [centimeters] out at the far end and let sit. Repeat until the belt is as wide as you want it.

Remove from Loom
Using a crochet hook, work along the warped edge taking the first two loops off their nails onto the hook. Pass the first loop over the second to begin binding off, just as you would in finishing a crochet project. Work down the length of the loom until this side of the belt is completely off the nails. For the last loop, pull the closest weft yarn through the loop and tie a knot. (This edge will be sewn to the leather, so it doesn't need to be pretty!) Trim the weft edge of the belt leaving a 1" (2.5 cm) seam allow-

Consider using studs or another decorative surface treatment to cover up structural stitching.

ance. On the other long side, tie alternating yarns together in knots so they don't slip through the weaving.

Note: Some of the fringe along the long edge will get tucked into the bind-off. This is good; it makes a dense, strong edge that will support the belt. Pull out fringe, as desired, for a decorative element.

Make the Belt

There are a hundred variations you could do here. The easiest is to cut a long piece of soft leather the same dimension as the weaving, place weaving on top of the leather, and sew them together along the short edge. Finish the edges with a zigzag stitch.

Loop one belt end through both belt rings, fold over and stitch through both layers to secure the rings in place. Add studs as a decorative element by piercing the leather with a leather punch and inserting the studs. Tighten the studs with needle-nose pliers. (Flat studs can be hammered.)

Aurora's Belt

Aurora used a piece of vintage weaving, which she trimmed to the same size as the leather. She then sewed both together using a zig-zag stitch. She sewed the weaving directly to the vintage material and leather, then hid the sewing with the pyramid studs.

Whole-Fleece Scarf with Lanolin

This is a great project for the time when you have a large, beautiful fleece and you want to make something grand from it. The size of this scarf will depend on the size of the fleece, so be prepared to go big!

Knitting Skills Required
Cast on (CO)
  Stockinette stitch (St st): knit RS rows, purl WS rows
  Reverse Stockinette stitch (Rev St st): purl RS row, knit WS rows.
  Bind off (BO)

Size
Length: 84" [2.1 m] without fringe
Width: 13" [33 cm]

Materials
About 32 oz [91 g] whole fleece yarn, about 12 wpi
Size 13 [9 mm] needles

Gauge
About 8 sts = 4" [10 cm] using size 13 [9 mm] needles in stockinette stitch

Fiber Prep
Wash your fleece according to the directions on page 19 for preparing a greasy fleece. You want to remove the dirt but preserve the lanolin. Once your fleece is washed and dried, put the fiber you are ready to spin into a black garbage bag and place in the sun or a warm place. The fleece will warm up in the bag liquifying the grease and making it very easy and quick to spin! If the locks don't separate easily, try loosening the fiber in a picker or by hand.

Note: Avoid putting really greasy fleece through your carder!

Spin!
Spin all of your batts as bulky thick-and-thin singles. Soak and set the twist.

Scarf
CO 22 sts.
    To keep the scarf from rolling in on itself alternate blocks in St st and Rev St st. Don't over-think the number of rows per block, just make them slightly different each time. This will lend an organic feel to the look of this scarf.

At 28" [71.1 cm] from CO edge, or one-third of the way through the scarf, gradually add 3 or 4 more sts to the rows. Heavy scarves tend to thin out in the middle after wearing and this will help compensate for that. Then at 56" [142 cm] from CO edge, or two-thirds of the way through, gradually decrease these 3 or 4 sts. Continue until 84" [2.1 m] from CO edge, or until you knit through all your yarn. BO.

Fringe
Cut sixteen pieces of yarn, each 14" [35.5 cm] long. Tie eight pieces evenly spaced along the CO edge; repeat for the BO edge.

Alternating blocks in knit and purl will keep this scarf from curling in on the edges.